THE REVOLUTION OF 1936–1939 IN PALESTINE BACKGROUND, DETAILS, AND ANALYSIS

GHASSAN KANAFANI

First published in July 2023 by
1804 Books, New York, NY

1804Books.com

The Revolution of 1936–1939 in Palestine © Copyright by Anni Kanafani. All rights reserved. Other selections © 1804 Books, New York, NY

ISBN: 978-1-7368500-4-6
Library of Congress Control Number: 2023942418

Originally published in "شؤون فلسطينية" *(Palestinian Affairs)* Issue #6 (January 1972). This translation is prepared from the text's publication in Arabic in the volume الدراسات السياسية المجلّد الخامس *(Ghassan Kanafani's Political Studies)* by Rimal Books, with permission from Ghassan Kanafani's heirs.

Translated by Hazem Jamjoum
Introduction by Layan Sima Fuleihan
Afterword by Maher al-Charif
Cover by Hannah Priscilla Craig

TABLE OF CONTENTS

The Palestinian Cause is a Banner for All of Humanity   v
by Layan Sima Fuleihan

The Revolution of 1936–1939 in Palestine

    Introduction   1

    Background: The Workers   5

    Background: The Peasants   15

    Background: The Intellectuals   23

    The Revolution   39

Ghassan Kanafani:
Pioneer in the Study of the Great Palestinian Revolution of 1936–1939   75
by Maher al-Charif

Glossary   81

Contributors   93

Acknowledgments   95

Endnotes   97

THE PALESTINIAN CAUSE IS A BANNER FOR ALL OF HUMANITY

In Lebanon, 1969, while Ghassan Kanafani sat down at his desk and embarked on the political and analytical study of the 1936–1939 Revolution, the center of the Palestinian armed struggle was coming to his doorstep. With it came major shifts for the entire region, and for his own political life.

That November, Yasser Arafat, the head of the Palestine Liberation Organization (PLO), and Emile Bustani, the commander of the Lebanese Army, arrived in Cairo at the invitation of Egyptian President Gamal Abdel Nasser to sign the Cairo Agreement; an accord that acknowledged the sovereignty of the Palestinian resistance and its right to carry out operations from Lebanese soil, as well as its right to administer the daily life of the thousands of Palestinian refugees within Lebanese borders. "The two delegations affirm that the Palestinian armed struggle is an act that comes in the interest of Lebanon," they wrote, "as it does in the interest of the Palestinian revolution and all Arabs."[1] The Cairo Agreement intended to put an end to the growing conflicts between the Lebanese Army and the armed sections of the PLO, giving space not only for the coordination of guerrilla operations against the Israeli occupation, but also for the development of social and political institutions that were necessary to sustain the resistance, institutions that would be indispensable for building a sovereign Palestinian state. Lebanon was soon to become the base of operations for the Palestinian resistance, in all of its forms.

The signing of the Cairo Agreement occurred at a moment of turmoil and regeneration for the region. It was a mere two years after the 1967 war—a war that not only resulted in the tragic defeat of the Arab forces, the further theft of Palestinian land by the expanding Zionist state, the strengthening of the Israeli settlement movement, and a crushing blow to the burgeoning Arab nationalist regional movement—it also created a new mechanism for imperialist invasion and aggression in the region, marking the first time a United Nations (UN) member state would justify initiating military conflict using the threat of anticipated attack; a tactic indispensable to the imperialist playbook in the region still today.*

Although the region had suffered a crushing defeat at the hands of imperialism, new and advanced strategies of resistance were emerging, and Ghassan Kanafani played a key role in this process. The forces of the Arab Nationalist Movement (ANM) were forced to retreat and were no longer supported by the mass wave of public optimism after their defeat in 1967. In the context of this retreat, the Arab Nationalist Movement reorganized. Under the leadership of George Habash, the people involved with the Movement founded the Popular Front for the Liberation of Palestine (PFLP), a Marxist–Leninist political party that took up both armed and ideological struggle. Kanafani was a central figure in this new organization, being elected to the Politburo and being appointed as the party spokesperson in 1969. That same

---

* Israel's claim of self-defense in 1967 would later be refuted thanks to the declassification of documents that proved it to be the initiator of that war (which claimed tens of thousands of Arab casualties and displaced over 300,000 Palestinians from their territories in only a few days). However, this false justification continues to serve as a precedent in the arena of international law and governance, paving the way for the US and its allies to justify military aggressions and economic coercions as preventative actions to avert a greater threat—a method that is all too familiar to a world that witnessed the devastating destruction of Iraq based on the mythical evidence of weapons of mass destruction. (See *The Six-Day War and Israeli Self-Defense: Questioning the Legal Basis for Preventive War* by John Quigley.)

year, he drafted the party program that officially adopted Marxism–Leninism, and founded the Party's newspaper, *Al-Hadaf (The Target)*.

Not coincidentally, the moment of consolidation in 1969 shared many characteristics with that period that is under Kanafani's analytical review in the following pages. The 1936–1939 Revolution was a period brief in time but nonetheless, one which, in the words of one of Kanafani's major references, Dr. Abdul-Wahhab Kayyali, "represented the highest stage of the Palestinian Arab struggle against the anti-Zionist convergence, and in which the weaknesses of the Palestinian Arab struggle were exposed."[2] According to Kanafani and his revolutionary contemporaries, the revolution of 1936–39 was one of the most concentrated and intense political experiences that would consequently set the conditions for the founding of the Zionist state of Israel as well as shaping the possibilities for the Palestinian liberation struggle. Kanafani's seminal study of this period has circulated in many languages, serving as a reference for the international movement against Zionism to better understand both the origins of the Zionist state and the major obstacles that have conditioned the Palestinian path forward.

Despite the wide circulation of this analytical historical text, Ghassan Kanafani is mostly remembered in the English-speaking world for his literary work (such as his fictional texts *Men in the Sun* and *Return to Haifa*). The wealth of his political work has not been translated from Arabic and it is rarely commented upon even in the world of Arabic letters. This may be partly because of the sheer quantity of writings that Kanafani produced in his thirty-six years under his name and the various pseudonyms he employed. There is also the reality that much of his writing, particularly his journalistic pieces, requires contextual knowledge that has been stolen from later generations. Kanafani didn't just write—he went to battle with his pen, deploying his sharp and cutting satire to expose opportunism, normalization, or betrayal of the revolutionary cause. Our generation is now tasked with recovering his analysis, including learning to read his journalistic and analytical texts, to build a full picture of his vision for Palestinian emancipation.

But this emphasis on his literary work in the consciousness of today's younger generation does not mean that his political insights are not well represented. On the contrary, it is impossible to separate his political and literary work. This is not simply because of the obvious truth that all writing is, of course, a political act. It is that his literary work achieves something that transcends the categories of both analysis and fiction: his words bring the reader to occupy the very human heart of his characters, and his characters are at once representative of the Palestinian experience, and at the same time, utterly and irrefutability human in their stubbornness to become an archetype. He gives his characters a freedom that cannot be restrained, even as he forces us to witness their displacement, imprisonment, inhumane suffering, and death. The stories he tells challenge us to confront our own humanity and to never separate our political perspective from the contradictory and complicated reality of what it is to be a human who loves, fears, despairs, dreams; a human who must navigate pride and shame, sacrifice, and survival, and who, with all of this complexity, is directly confronting the immense trauma and direct violence of colonial genocide.

Perhaps Kanafani's writing has this power because of the intense sensitivity with which he lived his life. There are countless biographies and reflections of his too-brief life. Nearly all cannot avoid mentioning the strength of his empathy and compassion, and his curiosity for the conditions of others. These qualities drove his political activity—political activity for which he would be martyred only a few years later by Zionist intelligence forces, forever remembered as "the commando who never fired a gun."[3]

❊ ❊ ❊ ❊ ❊

Ghassan Kanafani was born in 1936 in Acre, Palestine, a Palestine bubbling with anti-colonial activity. His father, a middle-class lawyer, was an active participant in the strikes of what became known as the 1936–1939 Revolution, and that Kanafani would study years later. At twelve years of age, he and his family were torn away from their home and their way of life by the violence of the Nakba, the Catastrophe, and made refugees in Syria. In this moment, Kanafani entered the world of the proletariat, the world of constant work and precarity. Like many of the displaced, his father struggled to find work as a refugee for material and psychological reasons alike, and so Kanafani and his siblings began to work as children to help support their family.

Kanafani continued his education while working. He enrolled in Damascus University to study Arabic Literature, which, due to his early education in French missionary schools, was difficult for him. His studies pushed him to develop mastery over the Arabic language with intention and curiosity, which perhaps contributed to his incredible ability to weave words with complexity and sensitivity. Soon he was expelled for his political activity with the ANM and continued his studies and political life in Kuwait, finally arriving in Beirut in 1960.

In Syria, Kanafani began work as a teacher in the schools run by the United Nations Relief and Works Agency (UNRWA) that had been built in the Palestinian refugee camps. In the UNRWA schools, he was confronted by the experiences of his students, many of whom faced extreme violence during and after their displacement. This period dramatically sharpened his class consciousness, and he would refer to this experience as fundamental to his political and literary development. His political development, and his way of approaching political analysis, always started with the concrete conditions of the people around him. In the same way, his path to Marxism–Leninism was not a direct one. He reached the conclusions in an organic way, his political instinct spurred by his emotional response to what he lived and witnessed, and sharpened by the influence of a range of people: the communist husband of his sister Fayzah, Husayn Najim; Dr. George Habash, who led the PFLP; and other Arab Nationalists and revolutionaries he encountered along the way.

In a sense, his political development was intertwined with that of the movement in which he was embedded. The Arab Nationalist

Movement was not explicitly socialist when he joined, and in fact, older members of the movement held some suspicion against socialist and communist ideas that, in Kanafani's assessment, was not due to any ingrained anti-communist principles, but rather due to the many mistakes made by the communist parties of the region at the time. But as it advanced its struggles against colonialism, the Movement could not avoid confrontation with the question of class and class struggle:

> The Arab Nationalist Movement was [directed] against colonialism, imperialism, and reactionary movements. It did not have an ideological line at that time. However, this movement adopted a socialist line of its own during the years it existed. Anti-imperialism gives impetus to socialism if it does not stop fighting in the middle of the battle and if it does not come to an agreement with imperialism. If this is the case, that movement will not be able to become a socialist movement. But if one continues to struggle [it is natural] that the [anti-imperialist] movement will develop into a socialist position. The Arab nationalists realised this fact in the late 1950s. They realised that they could not win the war against imperialism unless they relied on certain [social] classes: those classes who fight against imperialism not only for their dignity, but for their livelihood. And it was this [road] that would lead directly to socialism.[4]

This organic Marxism, generated by the conditions of struggle themselves, shines in all of Kanafani's writing. He produced an immense quantity of work, at a rate difficult to comprehend. He wrote constantly for various newspapers, sometimes under his own name, sometimes under others, and encouraged others to write and publish their perspectives as well. His writing, however, considered not just politics, economics, strategy, or analysis, but also, sometimes to the surprise of his contemporaries, culture. As editor of *Al-Hadaf*, he not only maintained the sections for cultural criticism and debate, but also identified emerging talents in cultural areas and opened platforms for the development of their voices.

We can see this commitment in the text translated in the following pages, which, alongside a thorough and detailed materialist analysis, includes a significant investigation into the forms of cultural expressions across sectors of society and from different class positions. It considers culture to be both a measure of political sentiment, activation, and participation, as well as an instrument that is, as he argues, often a much more effective mobilizing force than a political slogan when it comes to the Palestinian context. He gives the same thorough and rigorous attention in other works to the cultural production of the Zionists, taking on one of the first investigations of Zionist literature[5] to give more precise insight into the Zionist strategic and tactical approach on all fronts.

Kanafani's consideration of all dimensions of human life and society at all times is nothing more or less than a revolutionary commitment. The following text is materialist to its core, a true example of rigorous class analysis. But Kanafani is not one to use a mechanical definition of class. His definitions of class, class position, and class oppression begin with and return to the particular conditions of the Palestinian context, and consider the unquantifiable aspects of colonial oppression to identify with precision the class contradictions that will generate openings for struggle. And the analysis itself is not done for its own sake. His concern, again, is not to justify predefined positions, but to find where political and organizational leadership may have mistakenly identified the revolutionary sectors of society, or were misguided in their forms of communication, or were disconnected from the very masses that the Palestinian liberation movement is committed to defending. It is easy to understand the urgency with which Kanafani must have taken on this kind of historical evaluation, considering the context of defeat and reorganization in which he wrote.

With this political clarity, he makes it evident that the core contradiction characterizing the Palestinian struggle is not simply one of poor against the rich, nor Palestinian against European settler, nor Arab against Jew. It is the colonized against the colonizer in its fullest and most rigorous definition, one that considers the full complexity of class exploitation and class relations, national oppression, and the geopolitical correlation of forces; the colonized against a colonizer that wields the might of imperialism's unconditional support. Only with this clarity of analysis can we correctly assess the true obstacles confronting the Palestinian cause, which along with the Zionist colonial project include the Arab landowning and ruling classes inside Palestine and across the region, the British, and, now more than ever, the United States and its imperialist project of global hegemony. And only with this clarity can we correctly assess the forces of resistance, which include the Palestinian peasant class, the landless, the workers, the intellectuals and artists who take the side of the proletariat, the Arab masses and their organizations, socialist and communist parties, and the international working class positioned against imperialism in all contexts and forms.

With this clarity, Kanafani guides us to resist the isolation of the Palestinian cause as simply an issue for the Palestinians alone, or for the Arab states alone. When Zionism is understood as an imperialist project in its origin and its agenda, it becomes an enemy of all of humanity, and the Palestinian cause a banner for all of humanity.

❖❖❖❖❖

Kanafani is irrefutably more than just a writer: he is a militant and a political leader who wages struggle with his writing. In that sense, his writing is not just an archival document—it should be considered in all of its dimensions, especially when read and studied by those also engaged in struggle. Kanafani consulted the 1936–1939 Revolution, which ended in defeat, in a moment of another defeat during which the forces of resistance were reorganizing to adapt to new conditions. Just as "Lenin consulted Marx"[6] in pivotal times, so Kanafani consulted history, seeking from it a lived example to better understand a living reality. For us today, especially those of us who find ourselves in another moment of significant defeat and reorganization, we should consult Kanafani, and read his text not simply as an analysis of an experience almost a century ago, but as a source from which to glean certain key lessons for revolutionary movement today.

At the time of this writing, we have marked the seventy-fifth year of the Nakba. The Zionist occupation has yet again showered Gaza with bombs, murdering entire families. The most right-wing forces in the history of the Zionist project have entered the Israeli government, giving strength to the settler movement and escalating operations on the occupied Palestinian territories in their entirety, as well as the Lebanese and Syrian territories. Zionism does not only seek the borders of Palestine, it reaches beyond, pushing for an escalation of the US imperialist hybrid war in the entire region, and collaborating with right-wing and imperialist forces around the world.

At the same time, new forms of Palestinian resistance and international solidarity are surging, and the legitimacy of the Zionist project is rapidly disintegrating across the world. Today, after the COVID-19 pandemic and the rising waves of right-wing violence pulled away the last threads of capitalism's mask, and, on a geopolitical level, as concrete moves are being made to build alternatives to US military, political, and economic domination—the working and poor majority of the world are becoming more aware of the Palestinian cause, recapturing the internationalist consciousness that was fractured in the rise of neoliberalism and the fragmentation of the socialist bloc. Just like 1969, our time now is one of defeat, violence, and also resistance—a rapidly changing conjuncture that is generating new forms and new waves of struggle, giving new life to the path toward socialism and internationalism that Kanafani and his comrades fought for.

Kanafani should be alive today, confronting this reality with us. But I will not end this introduction with a description of his death. A death he told a million times in his stories—death at the hands of a colonizer who cannot accept the humanity of the colonized, because, like the clarity of a polished mirror[7], it forces him to confront his own inhumanity. But there is no revolutionary thinker in the world who could be stopped by death. Kanafani's vision, sensitivity, and love for his people are carried in the continued life and work of his family, Anni, Fayez, and Laila Kanafani, in the steadfastness of the Palestinian people, and the solidarity of all people who will not allow the banner of Palestinian liberation to drop until it is achieved, fully, and without compromise.

Instead, I would like to end this introduction with a proposal to read Kanafani's text as if he is here, sitting across from you[8] and speaking with you, alive and well. Listen to this immense example of revolutionary commitment and sacrifice, just as you would a respected comrade. Pause and reflect, disagree and debate, and listen again, considering all the ways in which this conversation may change the way you perceive your own context, diagnose the strengths and weaknesses of the moment, and shift your own analysis of today. And then, jump back into the collective life that is international class struggle, with his famous words to encourage you:

> Imperialism has laid its body over the world. . . . Wherever you strike it, you damage it, and you serve the world revolution.[9]

—Layan Sima Fuleihan
2023

THE REVOLUTION OF 1936-1939 IN PALESTINE BACKGROUND, DETAILS, AND ANALYSIS

INTRODUCTION

In the years 1936–39, the Palestinian revolutionary movement was dealt a devastating blow by the three formations that have since evolved to become the major forces working against the people of Palestine: reactionary Palestinian leaders, Arab regimes surrounding Palestine, and the alliance between Zionism and imperialism. This "enemy" triumvirate has left its imprint on the history of the Palestinian liberation movement most clearly from 1936 until the third defeat of the Palestinian and Arab masses in 1967. This study will attempt a particular focus on these three formations, and on the dialectical relations that comprise each of those formations as well as those existing between them.

The violence of the Palestinian national movement's experience—which has been in a state of eruption since 1918 and has included armed struggle in different ways at different times—did not manage to transform the movement's leadership. That leadership remained under the hegemonic control of semi-feudal/semi-religious leaders. There were two interconnected reasons for this.

First, the presence and effectiveness of the Zionist movement elevated the urgency and importance of the *national* cause above all other causes and struggles in Palestinian society. Indeed, the challenge posed by the Zionist movement imposed itself upon the Arab working classes, which had suffered directly and daily as a consequence of the British Empire-backed Zionist invasion.

The second reason was the presence of an abnormal limit acting upon the contradiction between British imperialism and the local Arab leadership composed of feudal-religious family patriarchs. Under the circumstances found in most other colonial contexts, such a leadership would ultimately find its class interests best served by a near-total alliance with imperialism. The abnormal particularity in the Palestinian case was the presence of a "more suitable collaborator" for British imperialism: the Zionist movement, who the Empire enlisted in place of the local ruling classes.

These two interwoven factors gave the Palestinians' struggle a specificity that made it, at that time, differ from the struggles of the Arab peoples across the region. This particularity had critical consequences. One such consequence was that this kind of feudal leadership took up, or tolerated the taking up of, the most advanced form of political struggle (the armed struggle). This leadership also put forward a progressive agenda, even if only at the level of lip service. Despite the role it ultimately played, it formed an important stage in the Palestinian struggle for freedom. More important than recognizing its actions, though, is explaining the abnormally long time that this feudal-religious leadership managed to remain at the helm of the mass popular movement (1918–48). The economic and social structural transformations in Palestine, which were taking place at a staggering speed, primarily affected the Jewish colonists' sector at the expense of the Arab working class in particular, as well as the Palestinian middle and petite bourgeoisie more generally. The transition from a feudal economy to a capitalist one took place through the accumulation and concentration of capital in the hands of the Zionist movement, and in the hands of Jewish communities in Palestine by extension. One of the results of this process was a remarkable phenomenon: Arab voices calling for conciliation began to make themselves heard in the 1930s and early 1940s, but they were not generally the voices of the landowners or middle peasants, but those of the upper echelons of the Arab urban bourgeoisie. This class had evidently begun folding its interests into those of the Jewish bourgeoisie, which was clearing a path toward industrialization and needed agents along the way.

The surrounding Arab countries played two two simultaneous but contradictory roles at this moment: at the same time that the movements of the Arab masses added strength to Palestinians' mass revolutionary spirit and worked to build mutually reinforcing relationships between the peoples and their struggles, the regimes dominating these societies did all they could to put an end to the movement of the Palestinian masses. This phenomenon is of great importance; the acute and compound nature of the contradictions, and how they played out on the Palestinian scene, promised to accelerate the development of the struggles on the other Arab scenes, elevating them to more sustained militant confrontation. This would broaden the range of revolutionary possibilities in Arab countries. The ruling classes in those countries had to take this very seriously, and it pushed them to consistently side with British imperialism against their class counterparts, who were leading the Palestinian nationalist movement.

The alliance between Zionism and imperialism grew steadily stronger. What developed dramatically in this period (1936–39) was not only the aggressive militarism of the invading society that had shoved its roots into the Jewish communities of Palestine, but also its near-total hegemony over Palestine's economic infrastructure. This was to have radical consequences on the struggle; in this period the Zionist leadership allied with the Mandate government against any hopes of a progressive Jewish labor movement, let alone any coming together of the Jewish and Arab proletariats. The Palestine Communist Party was sidelined by the working classes on each side of the colonial divide; the reactionary Histadrut took complete control of the Jewish labor movement; and the growing influence of progressive Arab forces in the Palestine Arab Workers' Society in Haifa and Yafa began to wane, ceding the ground to the reactionary leaderships that came to monopolize political action at the time.

BACKGROUND

THE WORKERS

Jewish immigration to Palestine and the difficulties it created were not solely moral or national matters; they had direct economic implications for the Arab population in Palestine, implications that were felt more and more acutely in the lived experience of each passing day, and especially by the small and middle farmers, workers, and certain sectors of the petite and middle bourgeoisie. The influx of migrants was in itself to have a major impact, one that was only compounded, naturally, by the national and religious character of the colonial migration. Between 1933 and 1935, 150,000 Jews immigrated to Palestine, growing the Jewish population to 443,000 people (29.6% of the total population). To appreciate these numbers we should put them in perspective. The average yearly number of Jewish immigrants to Palestine in the 1926–32 period was 7,201 people per year, and that this had effectively mushroomed to 42,985 Jewish immigrants per year in the 1933–36 period.[10] It was Hitlerian persecution that caused this dramatic increase in Jewish migration, a fact borne out by the preponderance of specifically German Jews moving to Palestine in those years of the Nazi rise to power: 9,000 in 1932; 30,000 in 1933; 40,000 in 1934; and 61,000 in 1935.[11] Almost three-quarters of the Jewish immigrants settled in Palestine's cities.

If responsibility for terrorizing Germany's Jewish communities lay with Hitlerism, it was "democratic" capitalism that, along with Zionism, was responsible for funneling those terrorized communities specifically to Palestine. This is confirmed by the figures: of the 2,562,000 Jews who managed to escape Nazi persecution between 1935 and 1943, the United States took in no more than 170,000 (6.6%), and Britain took in 50,000 (1.9%). It was left to Palestine to absorb 8.5%, while 1,930,000 German Jews (75.3%) took refuge in the Soviet Union.[12] We can get a sense of the seismic shock experienced by the Arab society of Palestine as a result of this migration by considering the proportion of the Jewish migrants who were capitalists: 11% (3,250 capitalists) in 1933; 12% (5,124 capitalists) in 1934; and 10% (6,309 capitalists) in 1935.[13]

The official statistics for the 1932–36 period show that 1,380 Jewish migrants entered Palestine with more than P£1,000 in these years, and 17,119 of the migrants were their dependents. Meanwhile, 130,000 were officially classified as either seeking waged employment, dependents of those seeking such employment, or dependents of pre-1932 migrants.[14] In other words, while the migration aimed to ensure that the agrarian-to-industrial transition of the "Palestinian" economy took place through capital concentrated in Jewish hands, it simultaneously aimed to provide this transition with a Jewish proletariat. These actions, manifesting under the slogan of "exclusively Jewish labor," had dire consequences, driving Jewish settler society in the direction of fascism at an exceptional velocity.

A fundamental contradiction between the Arab and Jewish proletariats was the inevitable result, extending not only to the Jewish peasants, farmers, and agricultural workers, but to the upper classes as well. The middle Arab landowners and urban bourgeoisie began to feel that Jewish capital was fast encroaching upon their interests. Already by 1935, Jewish capital controlled 872 of 1,212 industrial firms in Palestine, employing 13,678 workers compared to the 4,000 employed by Arab capital. Jewish investment that year totaled P£4,391,000 with production valued at six million Palestinian pounds, compared to the P£704,000 of Arab investment generating P£545,000. Moreover, the British Mandate government awarded 90% of its concessions to the

Jewish sector, which alone accounted for P£5,789,000 of state investment, underwriting the employment of 2,619 workers.[15]

The official census of September 1937 shows that Jewish workers' wages were, on average, 145% higher than those of their Arab counterparts in that year. This was much higher in particular sectors: the wage differential was 433% for women workers in textiles, 233% for women workers in tobacco sorting, 84% for typesetters, and so on.[16] "The real wages of the Arab worker witnessed a 10% decrease between 1931 and September 1937, while the real wages of the Jewish worker rose by 10%" over the same period.[17]

These economic effects of the Jewish migration became all the more dangerous as it became more evident that the British Mandate authorities had actively helped enable Jewish capital in the latter's bid to take control of Palestine's economic infrastructure; there was little hope of redress, let alone any hope of Palestinians becoming prime beneficiaries of future investments in infrastructure (roads, Dead Sea minerals, electricity, ports, etc.). These realities led to a near-total collapse of the Arab economy in Palestine, the brunt of which was borne by Arab workers. In his testimony to the 1937 Palestine Royal Commission (the Peel Commission), Secretary George Mansur of the Arab Workers' Society in Yafa reported that the standard of living for 98% of Arab workers was "far below the average." He went on to report that of one thousand Arab workers in Yafa surveyed by the Society in 1936, 57% earned less than P£2.75; 24% earned less than P£4.25; 12% earned less than P£6; 4% earned less than P£10; 1.5% earned less than P£12; and 0.05% earned less than P£15. The average minimum income required to support a family at the time was P£11.[18]

In the Arab Workers' Society's memorandum responding to the British authorities' refusal of a permit for a demonstration on December 6, 1935—organized by over one thousand unemployed workers in Yafa— the society warned that if the government did not take action to solve the problem, "the coming days would force it to choose between feeding the workers bread or bullets."[19] Revolution, at that point, was at the gates.

George Mansur—a former Communist who seems to have left the Party as its role diminished—presented the Peel Commission with an astounding sense of Palestinian workers' lived experience: by the end of 1935, Yafa alone had 2,270 unemployed male and female workers—a very large number for a city of 71,000 people.[20] Mansur identified five key factors underpinning the high unemployment rate, four of which were inseparable from Zionist immigration: (1) the economic effects of the immigration itself; (2) the growing pressures on peasants to move to the cities; (3) dismissal of Arab workers from waged work; (4) the overall deterioration in economic conditions; (5) the government's flagrant discrimination in favor of Jewish workers.[21] It is important to note that the experience in the Jewish sector was markedly different: in the first nine months of 1936, Histadrut membership grew by 41,000 workers.[22]

The result here was not only rising unemployment—as Arab workers lost their jobs in firms and projects that came under the control of Jewish capital—but also bloody confrontations. In four Zionist settlements alone (built on the lands of the Palestinian villages of Mulabbis, Deiran,* Wadi Hunain, and Khudaira) the number of Arab workers dropped from 6,214 in February 1935 to 2,276 Arab workers six months later, and then to only 677 Arab workers after about a year.[23] Violent attacks on Arab workers were also carried out, such as the Jewish garrison's assault on an Arab contractor and his workers to force them off their work on the construction of the Brodski building in Haifa in 1934. These systematic efforts to eliminate jobs held by Palestinians targeted Arab workers in the orchards, cigarette factories, construction sites, lime quarries, and others.[24] Between 1930 and 1935, Arab revenues from mother of pearl crafts, for example, dropped from P£11,532 to P£3,777. The number of soap

---

* Translator's note: It is unclear whether this refers to Deir Aban (on which the Zionist settler colonies of Tzora, Mahseya, Beit Shemesh, and Yish'i were built) or Khirbet Deiran (on which the Zionist settler colony of Rohovot was built). The major settler colony on the site of Mulabbis is Petah Tikva; the one on the site of Wadi Hunain is Ness Ziona, and the Hadera settler colony is on the site of Khudaira.

factories in Yafa alone dropped from twelve in 1929 to four in 1935. In 1930, these factories' exports were valued at P£206,259 plummeting to P£79,311 by 1935.[25]

The most apt description of the situation at the time described the Arab proletariat as "the victim of British colonialism and Jewish capitalism, with the primary responsibility falling on the former."[26] Yehuda Bauer adds to this analysis, stating that Palestine "on the eve of the 1936 disturbances was the only country in the world, excepting the Soviet Union, largely unaffected by the global economic crisis. Quite the contrary, it had experienced real prosperity as a result of the large influx of capital—over 30 million pounds sterling between 1932 and 1936—an influx that fell short of the investment opportunities arising from an ill-founded economic optimism."[27] This fragile economic efflorescence died down abruptly as soon as fear that war would break out in the Mediterranean caused an end to the inflow of private capital. As Bauer notes, "the credit system crumbled, signs of serious unemployment began to appear, and construction work died down. Arab workers were dismissed from their Jewish or Arab workplaces, and many returned to their villages ... the hammer of national propaganda had found in the economic crisis its anvil."[28]

As can be expected, Bauer's analysis whites out the most important factor: the rising rate of Jewish immigration to Palestine. Bauer's analysis appears unfounded in light of Sir John Hope Simpson's report of 1930, in which the British expert stated that "it would be a bad, and might prove a fatal policy, to attract large capital in order to start doubtful industries in Palestine, with the object of justifying an increase in the number of immigrants" (p. 117). In contrast to Bauer's statements, the influx of Jewish capital continued unabated in the years in question, reaching a peak in 1935. The rate of Jewish immigration also increased during these years, as did Jewish capital invested in Jewish industries and crafts which rose from P£5,371,000 in 1933 to P£11,637,300 three years later (p.313). Furthermore, the systematic dismissal of Palestinian workers from Jewish controlled workplaces had begun long before.[29] Meanwhile, droves of Arab peasants were uprooted and expelled from their lands and into the cities as a result of the Zionist colonization of the countryside.[30] According to some Israeli leftists, "the experience of fifty years does not contain a single example of Israeli workers being mobilized on material or trade union issues to challenge the Israeli regime itself; it is impossible to mobilize even a minority of the proletariat in this way."[31]

In fact, this was not a random, unexpected, or even unintended result of an otherwise meticulously drawn up plan. On the contrary, the Zionist leadership was fully aware of the consequences from the start. Decades earlier, Theodor Herzl himself had stated that "we must seize the privately held lands in the areas allocated to us from the landowners. The poorer inhabitants must be quietly moved beyond the borders by securing work for them in the countries to which they will relocate; we will deny them employment in our country. As for the landlords, they will join our ranks."[32] The Histadrut offers a clear formulation of the reality: "to allow the Arabs access to the Jewish labor market would mean that Jewish capital would be directed toward Arab development, and against Zionist objectives. Moreover, employment of Arabs in Jewish industry will lead to class divisions in Palestine along racial lines: Jews as capitalists using Arabs as laborers. We would thereby recreate in Palestine the same unnatural conditions that lead to the emergence of anti-Semitism in the Diaspora."[33] This congruence of settler colonial ideology and practice, together with the growing contradiction in its relation to the indigenous Arab communities, engendered fascist forms of Zionist organization, and this Zionist fascism borrowed methods from the Fascism then ascendant in Europe.

In this context the Arab worker was at the very bottom of the complex socio-political pyramid, and forced to bear its heavy weight. Matters only worsened as a result of the confusion in the fledgling Arab trade union movement. Between the early 1920s and the first years of the 1930s, the leftist workers' movement—both Arab and Jewish—suffered devastating blows that combined with the internal weakness of these currents to render them utterly debilitated. On one hand, the Zionist movement—hurtling as it was toward fascism and armed terrorism—posed a moral and material threat to the Communist Party. Despite its leadership being predominantly composed of Jewish activists, the Party was considered anathema to the Zionist movement, and especially to the movement's "labor" parties. On the other hand, the feudal-religious Palestinian leadership could not countenance the emergence of an Arab labor movement that operated beyond their own control (and a genuine labor movement could not possibly have emerged and developed under this leadership's control). This fledgling movement* was thus terrorized by the feudal leaders; in the early 1930s, the Mufti's thugs assassinated the head of the Arab Worker's Society in Yafa, Michel Mitri. Around a decade later, the head of the Society in Haifa, Sami Taha, was assassinated in the same way. Given the absence of a bourgeois force with political and economic influence, the political relationship between the workers and the feudal leaders was one of sharp antagonism, the intensity of which could only be resolved through a scenario in which the feudal-religious leadership took control of the workers' movement. Such a scenario, however, would mean that the revolutionary core of the labor movement would have been forfeited. Despite this antagonistic dynamic, there was always some common ground that could be found between the workers' movement and the interests of the feudal leadership in light of the conflagration of the national struggle.

---

* GK: The Arab Workers' Society, headquartered in Haifa, was established in 1925. In a very short period of time, it was able to set up 19 branches across Palestine (Akka, al-Bassa, Nablus, Tulkarem, Yafa, Lydd, Ramleh, Beit Nabala, Salama, Khan Yunis, Jerusalem, Imwas, Gaza, al-Majdal, al-Na'ani, al-Qubab, Tarshiha, and Safad). The Society's founding principles centered on organizing the workers, and defending them and their interests, they also included a clause stipulating that "all of [the organization's] activities will remain within the boundaries of law and order, and will not extend to political or religious matters." Despite this, the Society was able to mobilize broadly and powerfully. Its leadership was most often dominated by pan-Arabists, and many local revolutionary leaders emerged from its ranks. It is said that Izz al-Din al-Qassam had a powerful influence on the workers in the Society's rank and file.

The Communist Party's role in all of this was very important. One could perceive definite sparks of hope at the outset of the 1920s. In May 1921, for instance, around fifty-five communists held a demonstration in Tel Aviv and clashed with a Zionist rally. The communists were forced to flee Tel Aviv; they sought refuge in the Arab neighborhood of al-Manshiyah in Yafa where they were joined by the neighborhood residents in confronting the police who came to arrest the Bolsheviks.[34] A pamphlet distributed by the Communist Party's Executive Committee that same day stated that "Jewish workers live among you. They did not come here to oppress you but to live with you, and they are ready to fight alongside you against those moneyed enemies, be they Jewish, Arab or English. . . . If the holders of wealth incite you against Jewish workers to secure themselves against your retaliations, will you allow yourself to continually take the bait? The Jewish worker, a soldier in the revolution, has come to join his arms with yours as a comrade in the resistance against the English, Jewish and Arab capitalists . . . we call on you to fight the rich who have sold the country and its people to the foreigners. Down with the English and French lances, down with the Arabs and foreigners amassing fortunes. . . ."[35] What is astonishing in this long statement is not its abstract and fantastical analysis of the struggle, but also the fact that the word "Zionist" is completely absent in the text. In other words, the pamphlet completely avoided mention of the very thing that posed the danger felt by the Arab worker and peasant on a daily basis, the same danger likely felt by the fifty-five "Jewish" communists beaten up by the Zionists of Tel Aviv that morning.

The Palestine Communist Party would remain at this same distance from reality until 1930, at the end of which the Party held its seventh congress. In one of the resolutions passed at that meeting, the Party admitted that it had "adopted an erroneous attitude on the Palestinian national question, that is on the question of the role of the Jewish national minority in Palestine vis-à-vis the Arab masses. As a result, the Party had not carried out any activity among the Arab masses, confining itself to working exclusively among Jewish workers.

This self-isolating approach was reflected in the Party's position during the Arab uprising in 1929, in which the Party was effectively severed from the movement of the masses."36

Though the Party levied accusations against the Palestinian bourgeoisie (which itself was in a delicate position), and though the Party oriented itself away from tactics involving the building of popular fronts and alliances with revolutionary classes, the records of its seventh congress in 1930-31 offer some of the most valuable and forthright deliberations in the Party's history. According to those records, the discussions at that congress placed the prioritization of the Arab national question as a primary task of the revolutionary struggle, admitting that the Party's self-imposed distance from the movement of the masses was the "result of Zionist deviation that hindered the Arabization of the Party," and further admitted that it was "opportunist tendencies [that worked toward] halting any such Arabization of the Party." Having accepted this elementary reality, stating that it must work to expand the cadres of revolutionary forces (read: the cadres of revolutionary Arab workers) capable of directing the activity of the peasantry toward the correct path. Thus, the Arabization of the Party, that is, the transformation of the Party into the genuine party of the Arab working classes, is the primary and fundamental condition for "any successful activity in the rural areas."37

The Party, however, was in no way capable of carrying out its Arabization objective. As such, the correct revolutionary slogans it adopted at the congress could not move beyond the realm of abstraction. These slogans included "not a single dunam to the imperialist and Zionist usurpers"; "for the revolutionary expropriation of lands controlled by governments, wealthy Jewish colonizers, Zionist factions, and major Arab landowners and farmers"; "land sale agreements [to the Zionists] will not be recognized"; "we must fight against the Zionist usurpers." The congress resolved that "all major burning issues, and the end to oppression is only possible through an armed revolution under the leadership of the working class."38

The phrase "is only possible" was the important one.

The Palestine Communist Party did not accomplish its goal of Arabization. As a result, the entire edifice of its newfound strategy stood on shaky ground, leaving the field open to the domination of the feudal-religious leaders. There were numerous causes for this, but the most important of these was, perhaps, that the Party line reflected the uncompromisingly doctrinaire and revolutionary position for which the Comintern [Communist International] became famous between 1928 and 1934. Despite the small number of communists, their isolation, their lack of success at Arabizing the party, and their failure to mobilize in rural areas, they did in fact throw all they could muster into the battle that erupted in 1936; they took courageous stances, cooperated with some of the local leaders, supported the Mufti, many gave their lives, and many others were imprisoned. They were not, however, able to play an effective role. The slogan of Arabization seems to have gotten lost along the way, as partially evidenced on January 22, 1946 (ten years after the outbreak of the uprising), by Izvestia's brazen description of the "Jewish struggle" in Palestine as comparable to that of the Bolsheviks before the revolution of 1917.

It was only recently that the records of the Palestine Communist Party's seventh congress have become available, and the fact remains that the Arabization strategy was never actualized. Despite the Party's important role on the cultural level, and the contributions its members made on this front, the Party itself did not live up to the role in the Palestinian struggle that it had envisaged for itself at its seventh congress. The Party split during the 1936 Revolution, and split again in 1948, and again in 1965. Underlying each of these splits was the Arabization question, with those splintering away doing so on the basis of wanting to adopt a more "constructive" attitude toward Zionism. The result of the Communist Party's virtual absence from the political scene, the weakness of the rising Arab bourgeoisie, and the fragmentation of the Arab labor movement was that feudal-religious leaders were poised to play the leading role when events escalated toward the eruption of 1936.

BACKGROUND

THE PEASANTS

This was the situation of the workers' movement on the eve of the 1936 Revolution's eruption. However, this only gives us half the picture of the compound contradiction between the Jewish and Arab societies in Palestine, and *within* each one of those societies. The other half of the picture was in the countryside. It was in these rural areas that the struggle took on a manifestly national form. Jewish capital pouring into Palestine, together with the military forces of the British imperialists, and the immensely powerful English administrative apparatus had achieved pathetic results for the Zionist ambitions to create a Jewish state (a measly 6,752 colonizing settlers). They had, however, wrought serious damage upon the Arab masses: Jewish organizations' landownership rose, at the expense of both rural and urban property, from 300,000 dunams in 1929 to 1.25 million dunams in 1930. Though these 100,000 hectares were insignificant from the perspective of the mass colonization project (let alone the "solution to the Jewish question"), the expropriation of around one million dunams—about one-third of the arable land—entailed the impoverishment of the peasants and bedouin at an unprecedented scale and rate; the Zionists had expelled 20,000 peasant families by 1931.[39] The key point here is that in addition to this systematic impoverishment, this immiseration was unmistakably being carried out along primarily national lines. The agrarian in the underdeveloped world generally, and in the Arab world in particular, is not only a mode of production, but also the deep-rooted social, religious, and ritualistic way of life. As such, this violent dispossession took on a form that appeared primarily as a purely national confrontation. Up until 1931, only 151 of every thousand Jews in Palestine worked in agriculture, while 637 of every thousand Muslim Arabs worked in this sector. So, of the nearly 119,000 agricultural workers in Palestine, no more than about 11,000 were Jewish.[40] While agricultural workers comprised only 19.1% of the Jewish community, they made up 59% of the Arab community.

The economic basis for the intercommunal antagonism was, of course, critical. But to understand it properly we have to appreciate its national dimension. In 1941, 30% of the Arab peasants did not own any land, while 50% of the rest owned plots insufficient to sustain themselves. While 250 Arab feudal landowners owned four million dunams, 25,000 peasant families were landless, 46,000 peasant families were smallholders owning an average of 100 dunams per family, and 15,000 relied on waged agricultural labor for the landlords. A 1936 study of 322 Arab villages revealed that 47% of peasants owned less than seven dunams, 53% owned less than twenty dunams, while the minimum amount of land required to sustain an average family was thirteen dunams.[41]

As the Arab peasant suffered the triple nightmare of Zionist colonization of the land, Arab feudal landownership, and the exorbitant taxation levied by the British Mandate government, the challenge that took center stage was the national one. In the Intifadas of August 1929 and 1933, many of the Arab smallholders sold their lands to the large Arab landowners to buy weapons with which to fight Zionist colonization and British occupation. Colonialism—which threatened a way of life that encompassed aspects of religion, tradition and honor— enabled the feudal-clerical leaders to hold on to their positions of social leadership despite the crimes they continued to commit; in many cases, those same feudal elements buying the land from the smallholders went on to sell it to Jewish capital.

Between 1933 and 1936, 62.7% of the total land purchased by Zionists were lands owned by landowners who were physically present in Palestine, 14.8% were owned by absentee landlords, and 22.5% were the lands of smallholders. This was in sharp contrast to the 1920–22 period, when the proportion of Zionist land purchases were: 75.4% from absentee landlords, 20.8% from resident landlords, and 3.8% from smallholders.[42]

The laws passed by the Mandatory government were designed to serve the objectives of Jewish colonial settlement. Though these laws purported to include provisions guaranteeing protection for the Arab peasants against forced eviction and against being forced to sell, the reality was that no such protection was in place. This was clearly illustrated in the "case of Wadi al-Hawarith that had an area of 40,000 dunams, and the cases of the village of Shatta that had an area of 16,000 dunams, and many other such cases in which the Jewish settlers seized the lands and dispersed the Arab inhabitants. The result was that the 50,000 Jews living in agricultural settlements owned 1.2 million dunams, an average of 24 dunams per inhabitant. Arab peasants, in contrast, numbered 500,000 and owned less than six million dunams, averaging twelve dunams per inhabitant."[43] Another instance was that of the 8,730 peasants evicted from Marj ibn Amer (240,000 dunams), which was sold by the Beiruti feudal Sursuq family. The peasants' formal attempts to reclaim their land remained suspended between the offices of the Mandate government from the conclusion of the land deal in 1921 until the Mandate's end in 1948.[44]

"Every plot of land the Jews buy becomes alien to the Arabs, as if it were severed from the body of Palestine and transferred to another country."[45] Despite having expressed this moving sentiment, the major feudal landowner who uttered them, who would also play a leadership role in the Palestinian national movement, also stated that "the Jews say that 10 percent of the land they were sold was from peasants while the rest was from the major landowners." As if somehow irked by this, he goes on to assert that "the reality, however, is that 25 percent of the lands they were sold was from peasants."[46] There is some basis for this feudalist's sheepishness; Jewish land expert Granot [Avraham Granovsky] has attested to the fact that the holdings of the three largest Jewish landowning companies in 1936 (accounting for about half of the land acquired by Zionist bodies) was composed of: 52.6% lands purchased from major absentee landlords; 24.6% from resident large landowners; and 13.4% from state lands, churches, and foreign companies; and 9.4 from individual peasants."[47]

The land purchases created a fast-growing class of landless peasants, who could only eke out a livelihood in the countryside from seasonal waged agricultural work. As a result, most of them headed for the cities where they became cheap unskilled labor. There was no case in which "a peasant removed from his land went on to secure another plot of land, not a single one. Compensation was most often very meager, and only generous when it was the village *mukhtar* [mayor] or its notables."[48] The vast majority moved to the cities: "Most of the street cleaners in Yafa are from the villages (such as Barbara), and the Arab Tobacco and Cigarette Company in Nazareth reports that most of its workers are villagers, or of village origin."[49] We get a clearer picture when we consider the following description: "We asked the [Arab Tobacco and Cigarette Company] about how many workers it employs, to which the answer was 210. We then asked how much it paid in total weekly wages, to which the answer was P£62. If we divide that amount by the number of workers, we get an average weekly wage per worker of 29 piastres."[50] The weekly wage of a female Jewish worker in the tobacco industry at the time ranged from 170 to 230 piastres.[51] This disparity in pay extended to public sector jobs: a landless Arab peasant who moved to the city and found a government job, at the department of public works for instance, would usually be paid less than half the wage of his Jewish counterpart.[52]

The Johnson-Crosby Commission estimated the Arab peasant's yearly pre-tax income in 1930 at P£31.37. The same report, which estimated a peasant family's subsistence income at P£26, showed that the average peasant paid three sets of taxes amounting to P£3.87. If we also factor in the P£8 that the average peasant paid as interest on his debts, we find that the average peasant family lived on P£19.5 per year, well below subsistence. "The peasant class was in fact the only class obliged to help raise all the types of taxes in Palestine . . . the policy pursued by the government aims to place the peasant in an economic position that ensures the establishment of a Jewish national homeland."[53]

The direct effects of Jewish immigration—as well as the important related process of transforming the "Palestinian" economy from an Arab agrarian economy to a Jewish industrial one—were primarily felt by the Arab smallholding peasant. The extortionist tax burden on these peasants was geared toward offsetting the government revenues lost to tax exemptions enjoyed by Jewish immigrants, as well as those designed to encouraging Jewish industry: high tariffs on retail imports and lowered import tariffs on raw materials, unfinished goods, coal, packaging materials, etc. Import tariffs on retail goods rose from 11% at the start of the Mandate to 26% in 1935, with a 100% increase on sugar, 149% on tobacco, 208% on petrol, 400% on matches, and 26% on coffee.[54]

A story told by Bishop Gregorius Hajjar to the 1937 Peel Commission sums up the condition of the economically beleaguered peasant in a succinct and symbolic way:

> While in the village of al-Rameh in the Akka district one time, I heard the complaints of the inhabitants of the village and its surrounding area, which have the biggest harvest season for olives and pure olive oil. Long had the residents submitted complaints to the High Commissioner about the Shemen oil company's use of industrial oils. The company's operations were favored by the government in that they were exempted from paying customs duties on the peanuts from which they extracted oil that was then mixed in with olive oil and sold at extremely low prices. The villagers persisted in repeatedly submitting complaints,

requesting that the oil they produced be protected. The government responded by forming a committee tasked with hearing the villagers' complaints. When the committee arrived at al-Rameh, the villagers were furious to find that the committee was headed by none other than the director of the Shemen company himself.[55] ... It is not only sad, but outrageous, that the taxes in Palestine are imposed on the classes of the population as follows: a man whose annual harvest yields P£23.37 pays 25% in taxes, whereas the combined taxes for a merchant or member of the free professions whose annual income is P£1000 is 12%.[56]

The small and middle peasants were battered by such policies. The resulting impoverishment and land loss were seriously aggravated by Zionist practices embodied in the slogans of "exclusively Jewish labor" and "buy only Jewish products." Further compounding this immiseration was not only that it led Jewish agricultural and industrial employers to hire exclusively Jewish laborers and pay them higher wages, those higher costs of production were born by lower and middle Palestinian classes in the form of higher prices on an array of essential goods. The campaign for the Hebraization of production encouraged Jewish inhabitants to choose Jewish-produced goods over lower priced Arab alternatives.[57]

If we keep in mind what we have seen before, that most raw materials were exempted from import duties, and that such duties were quite high on retail imports which could compete with goods produced by Jewish manufacturers in Palestine, it becomes clear that the costs of Hebraization of labor policy were primarily borne by the poorer classes of the Arab population. On the flipside of this was the class that came to be known as the *effendiyya*, who lived in the urban centers and whose income predominantly derived from the agricultural land they leased to the peasants, and from the interest on loans to the peasantry. In the 1930s, the *effendiyya* had not yet begun to invest in industry or urban-based crafts (something they would begin to do in a limited way in the 1940s). The extortionism of the *effendiyya*, however, appeared to the peasants as the less ruinous evil when compared to the harm that Zionism entailed.

There is another "class" that has not been given enough attention in Palestinian studies: the bedouin "class." The number of bedouin in Palestine had dropped from 103,000 in 1922 to 66,553 in 1931. This part of Arab society, which played a prominent role in the 1936 Revolution, had come to the attention of the Communist Party (at the seventh congress discussed above) through their important participation in the August 1929 intifada. The bedouin, who made up around 35% of the population, endured "near constant hunger, which puts them in a state of rage consistently teetering on the edge of armed rebellion. Their participation in the August uprising is evidence of the major role they can play in a revolutionary insurrection of the masses. At the same time, it is clear that the sheikhs and leaders of these tribes can be corrupted by money . . . the bedouin unceasingly provide new hands and voices to an army of landless peasants and semi-proletarians."[58]

The fragmented Arab urban bourgeoisie was, meanwhile, in a state of confusion, loss, and disarray. The speed at which the society was transitioning into one dominated by Jewish industrial capital gave no chance to either the fledgling bourgeoisie or the feudalists to take part in or profit from this transition. As such, it was not at all strange to see the Palestinian leaders who testified before the 1937 Peel Commission, and similar commissions prior, heaping flattery upon the Ottoman Empire, praising its treatment of them in comparison to their treatment at the hands of the British: they had been an instrument of the Sublime Porte, an arm of the Sultan, an integral part of Ottoman hegemony, exploitation and repression. The British Empire had dismissed them from the post of agent-in-chief; in the Zionist movement it had found a more qualified, reliable, and organized henchman for the role.

These were the basic contours of the role to be played by the feudal-clerical leaders: a "struggle" for a better position within the colonial regime. They could not, however, wage such a "struggle" without assembling behind them the ranks of classes desperate to unyoke themselves of both the dual national oppression and the dual class oppression that had become so firmly entrenched. Not only did these leaders take up forms of struggle they would normally find anathema, they drew up a strategy far more progressive than their actual interests, appropriating the slogans of the masses that expressed goals the leaders were neither able to achieve, nor interested in actualizing. Though some like to suggest otherwise, the leaders did not have free rein to act as they pleased. They were constantly beset by all sorts of pressures and constraints shaping the course of events, by the ever-intensifying contradictions that often came to a head, and by the range of factors we have already discussed. This explains the partial contradictions that would arise between this feudal-clerical class and the regimes of the Arab states surrounding Palestine, regimes composed of this class's counterparts. It also explains this class's wide-ranging alliances within the different elements of the class structure in Palestine.

BACKGROUND

THE INTELLECTUALS

In his report of 1930, thirteen years into the British occupation of Palestine, the Director of Education stated that "since the beginning of the occupation, the government has never undertaken to provide sufficient funds for the building of a single school in the country." In 1935, the government rejected 41% of Arab applications for enrollment in schools. In eight hundred Arab villages in Palestine there were only 269 boys' schools, 15 girls' schools, and 15 girls from the villages who made it to the seventh elementary grade. None of the villages had a secondary school, and 517 villages had no school at all. On top of this, the government "censored books and worked against all cultural ties to the broader Arab world while doing nothing to improve social conditions among the peasantry...."[59] In 1931, and as a consequence of these policies, those attending school among Palestinian Muslims were 251 per thousand males and 33 per thousand females; 715 per thousand males and 441 per thousand females among Palestinian Christians; and 934 per thousand males and 787 per thousand females across the country's Jewish communities.[60]

Despite the disparity evidenced by these statistics, one that affected rural areas in particular, the numbers do not give a qualitative sense of the Arab cultural scene, which played a vanguard role from the very beginning of the Arab cultural resurgence (the Nahda) in the early twentieth century. In fact, numerous printing presses had been set up in Palestine before the British occupation, publishing around fifty Arabic-language newspapers established in the country between 1904 and 1922. By the time the revolution broke out in 1936, at least another ten newspapers were also being printed and circulated widely.

There are many factors that made Palestine an important Arab cultural center, and there is no space to expand upon all of them here. One key factor was the constant migratory flow of intellectuals to and from Palestine. Many of these traveling intellectuals helped establish literary societies and cultural clubs from the early 1920s onwards. Fed by a gushing stream of college graduates from Beirut and Cairo, this cultural development included a vibrant movement publishing Arabic translations of English and French texts. There is no doubt that foreign missionary societies, disproportionately active in Palestine due to its specific religious significance, played a prominent role in urban education. Despite the importance of appreciating the general cultural climate in Palestine of the 1930s, it is not our central concern here. What concerns us specifically is how this climate articulated and interacted with the worsening crises at the economic and national levels in ways that incited and mobilized people to act.

We can investigate these diverse articulations and interactions by studying the literary and cultural movement in Palestine at the time, and especially by examining the development of what we can describe as popular mass culture: that type of consciousness that grows in a countryside drowning in the kinds of ignorance bred by illiteracy, while forced by everyday challenges to be constantly on the alert. It is clear that the urban intellectuals, by and large, shared class backgrounds that set them apart from their rural counterparts. Despite generally belonging to feudal, mercantile, and petit bourgeois families, these members of the urban intelligentsia were driven by their circumstances at a critical juncture in their country's history to play a rather unique role: they were ostensibly calling for a bourgeois revolution, but this "bourgeois revolution," for which they were the vanguard, had no real material base that could translate into a movement with its own power and program. Hegemony of the political field was left to the feudalists, who did all they could to bring these intellectuals under their leadership (something that left an indelible imprint on intellectual activity). This actually created a context in which these intellectuals had greater freedom, for they were not fettered by the kinds of real material conditions that would constrain a bourgeoisie. This flexibility in the limits imposed by their actual class interests enabled them to be more progressive than their class and cultural counterparts among the poets and writers of other Arab countries in the same period.

In the countryside, the *qawwalun* (traveling poet musicians) drew from their constant interactions with the rural population to develop a kind of political *zajal* (sung poetry) that reflected the hopes and concerns of the peasantry, and in a way that kept pace with the exacerbation of their struggles, rooted in grievances that were growing more deeply and widely felt. In these areas, popular poetry in its various forms, is a hallowed ritual of life and a tradition that becomes even more deeply rooted over time. Taking form through countless contributions, and over extended periods of time marked by repeated social shocks and crises, popular poetry held the kind of power we now associate with mass media.

It is beyond the scope of this study to investigate the mechanics of mass communications, and by extension the nature of the complex and compound cultural confrontation between calls for revolution and calls for quietism (which take on a more complex and slower paced form in the underdeveloped rural setting). This said, it must be noted that many of those we assume would play a negative role (such as the mosque preachers, for example, who would be among the rural intellectuals with the greatest influence) did not completely perform in the way we might expect. At certain moments, the national and class contradiction reaches a point at which even the mosque's imam needs to justify his positionality; if such a justification does not lead to the direct positive results desired by the people, even the venerated man of religion can find his social status undermined. Given this dynamic, the revolutionary culture gained ground every day in the cultural struggle taking place between the revolutionaries and reactionaries in the countryside, and between the revolutionaries and the nihilists and romantics in the cities. We do not know of a single Palestinian writer or intellectual in the period under study who did not, to some extent, join in the call to resist the colonial enemy. It was only a tiny minority of poets who abstained from penning verses on the national question.

What we are talking about here is the general cultural climate in Palestine. Intellectuals played a role that was disproportionately active for such a social group—especially when we consider that they were not organized in and by political parties—when compared to similar groups reckoning with the classical conditions of a national liberation struggle. Indeed, the particularity of Palestinian intellectuals' position was unique when compared to Arab intellectuals writ large: in the city, the sons of the wealthy returned from their studies to find the class they belonged to standing completely impotent, unable to lead battle to which it had assigned itself command. They clearly perceived their own underdevelopment and cultural weakness in the face of the changing world around them, while also unable to find a place for themselves in the transition toward a modern society with an industrial character; the social force controlling that transition was, at heart and on the surface, foreign and alien. The only dominant bourgeoisie on the scene was not only one that confronted them at the national level, but also bore a culture that imposed itself as a negation of their own, and of their cultural aspirations more broadly.

In the countryside, the Palestinian peasant—who had for centuries languished under class and national oppression that had disfigured him into a creature of abject fatalism under the banner of religious loyalty—had established for himself a "cultural" world fenced in by traditions imposed by the dominant class. This power structure expressed itself through popular proverbs and sayings that took on a power akin to that of the law, a power familiar everywhere, and especially in rural areas under a feudal mode of production, "for [such proverbs and sayings] are not simply a form of folklore ... they are speech acts that lead to the most powerful form of influence on the course of events and everyday human practice."[61]

Abject poverty, crushing oppression, and centuries of class and national repression combined to establish the "perfect system" for defeatism, fatalism, and political quietism that was reflected in the most widespread popular proverbs and sayings.* It was up to the Palestinian intellectuals, and especially the popular poets in the countryside, to face the massive challenge of altering this culture of subservience while themselves still under its influence. In truth, a group of Palestinian intellectuals strove to do just that from the earliest stages of the Palestinian struggle, playing an important role in forming a progressive consciousness. The resulting relationship between both the vernacular popular poetry (as well as the classical [fus'ha] poetry of the cities) and the struggle was not one of mere description and documentation, but a deeply dialectical one.

One such intellectual was Wadi' al-Bustani. Of Lebanese origin, al-Bustani moved to Palestine after graduating from the American University of Beirut in 1907. In the same month in which the Balfour Declaration was issued in 1917, al-Bustani warned against its consequences with the clarity of a polished mirror. It is worthwhile to

---

* GK: Examples of such sayings include: He who eats from the Sultan's bread can strike with his sword; if you have a penny you can make a penny; a good bribe loosens a bad judge's purse strings; the mettle of men is in the lies they can tell; a thousand setbacks are better than a defeat; the only grass that matters is the grass on my side of the fence; an egg today is better than a chicken tomorrow; put your head with all the others before you tempt the headsman; don't stretch your toes beyond your blanket; the prince's dog is a prince; rice gets the glory and bulgur can go hang itself; move into the coffin business and people will stop dying; the worst of the pain is the pain right now; if you can't beat them join them; he runs after the loaf and the loaf just races ahead; the world stands with the one standing; only God decides on life and livelihood; a person in need is a burden; we were so poor the spit on the ground looked like a shilling; the eye does not rise above the brow; I'm the first to comply and the last to rebel.

look a bit more closely at the period represented by al-Bustani, and which would flourish in the leadup to the armed revolution in the 1930s through a vanguard of poets and rural singers who would stoke the flames of the armed uprising and make it integral to the popular heritage of the masses who saw the "prince's dog" as a prince. On December 29, 1920, the Mandatory government sent a letter to the owner and editor of the Haifa-based cultural periodical *al-Karmel* requesting that he publish a poem gifted to the High Commissioner by the celebrated Iraqi poet Ma'ruf al-Rasafi during the poet's visit to Palestine. In the poem, al-Rasafi glorified a Jewish preacher named Yehuda and heaped lavish praise on the British High Commissioner. The magazine editor found it unsuitable to publish the poem without a response. al-Bustani rose to the challenge, writing:

> The sermon of Yehuda? Or, an act of sorcery?
> The sayings of al-Rasafi? Or deceit in verse,
> Your prosody is of the rarest pearls among words
> And you are the one who knows best the pearls in poetry's sea
> But this sea is the sea of politics
> Where a high tide of justice demands its ebb
> True, he who crossed in from the Jordan is our cousin
> But our worry is about he who crossed in from the sea

This long poem, which became famous at the time, is in fact an important historical document; not only does it take al-Rasafi to task, it also confirms Palestinian intellectuals' positionality vis-à-vis the critical political variables in the early years of the struggle, including the Jewish immigration and the dangers it posed, the British role in pitting Arabs against one another, the Balfour Declaration and its pitfalls, and so on. On March 28, 1920, just a short time before the al-Rasafi incident, al-Bustani had led a demonstration with a poem he had written. The poet was summoned for interrogation by the public prosecutor, the records of which include the following:

Prosecutor: We received reports that you were carried above people's heads, chanting the words that the crowd repeated after you: "Oh Christians, Oh Muslims!"
The accused: Yes.
Prosecutor: [And you also said:] "Who have you vacated the country for?"
The accused: Yes.
Prosecutor: [You then said:] "Kill the Jews and the unbelievers…"
The accused: No. That distorts the meter and the rhyme, and what I said followed the meter and the rhyme, and also had meaning. They call it poetry."[62]

Poetry in particular would come to play an increasingly central role, deployed in all manner of occasions to express that which festered in the hearts of the downtrodden masses. When Balfour came from London to participate in the 1925 opening ceremony of the Hebrew University, Ahmad Lutfi al-Sayyid was also in attendance as an official representative of the Egyptian government. On that day, the poet Iskandar Khouri al-Beitjali directed these verses at Balfour:

> You came running from London to stoke the flames of this battle
> Oh Lord, I do not blame you for you are the source of this tragedy
> My blame is for Egypt, which extended her hands to us with a blow[63]

From the beginning of the 1930s, the poets Ibrahim Tuqan, Abu Salma (Abd al-Karim al-Karmi), and Abd al-Rahim Mahmoud represented the crest of a wave of patriotic poets whose work flowed all over Palestine, raising awareness and inciting the people to action.*

---
* GK: According to Tawfiq Zayyad, the resistance poet from occupied Palestine (Nazareth): "Our revolutionary poetry (by such poets as Mahmoud Darwish, Samih al-Qasim, and myself) is an extension of the revolutionary poetry of Ibrahim Tuqan, Abu Salma, Abd al-Rahim Mahmoud, Mutlaq Abd al-Khaliq, and others… because our battle is an extension of their battle." ("On literature and popular Palestinian literature" Beirut: Dar al-Awda, 1970, p. 14).

Other notable intellectuals and poets in this tradition include: Is'af al-Nashashibi, Khalil al-Sakakini, Ibrahim al-Dabbagh, Muhammad Hasan Ala' al-Din, Burhan Abboushi, Muhammad Khurshid, Qaisar al-Khouri, George Bitar, Boulos Shehadeh, Mutlaq Abd al-Khaliq, and others.

The work of Tuqan, al-Karmi, and Mahmoud displays an astounding appreciation of what was happening around them that can only be explained as a profound understanding of what the masses were feeling. What appears in their poems as inexplicable prescience and prophecy, as if drawn from some mystical oracle, was no more than an uncanny ability to express that dialectical relationship between their artistic output and the spirit of the movement spreading throughout Palestinian society.

We can offer one example from the work of Ibrahim Tuqan. He produced a poem in 1932 to comment upon the establishment of the "National Fund" to save Palestinians' land from sales to Zionist bodies. The Fund was established by the feudal-clerical leadership under the pretext of alleviating the pressure on poorer peasants to sell their land. According to Tuqan: "Eight of those leading the project to establish this fund were themselves brokers of land sales to the Jews:"

> If only a leader of ours would fast
> Like Ghandi, for his fast might do good
> He won't abstain from food; in Palestine a leader dies if it weren't for his food
> May he fast from selling land
> A spot he can save to rest his bones [64]

Our focus on the role played by poetry and popular poetry is not meant to suggest that other forms of cultural production in Palestine did not play any role, nor that this role was marginal. Journalism, literary essays, stories, and the translation movement collectively played a very significant leadership role. For example, the opening editorial published by Yusuf al-Isa in a 1920 issue of *al-Nafa'is* stated: "Palestine is Arab, Arab through its Muslims, Arab through its Christians, Arab in its patriotic Jews. On what basis does the Zionist foreigner sell it off . . . the storms of Palestine will not quiet if it is severed from Syria and rendered a national home for Zionism. . . ."

These initial efforts, beginning in the early 1920s, fashioned the rising tide of the revolutionary culture in the 1930s that played a key role in the development of popular consciousness and the eruption of the revolution. These intellectuals working in forms other than poetry included: Arif al-Arif; Khalil al-Sakakini, the caustic and daring prose-writer and son of a master carpenter; Is'af al-Nashashibi, a member of the haute bourgeoisie who was so heavily influenced by al-Sakakini that he adopted some of his ideas as his own; Arif al-'Azzuni, Mahmud Saif al-Din al-Irani; Najati Sidqi, the early leftist voice who, in 1936, lauded Ibn Khaldun's materialism, openly despised idealism, and may have been the first to offer a materialist history of the Arab patriotic movement from the beginning of the Nahda, publishing his findings in Al-Tali'a in 1937–38; Abdullah Mukhlis, who insisted on a class analysis of colonialism from the mid-1930s, as well as on committed artistic production; Raja Hourani; Abdullah al-Bandak; Khalil al-Budairy; Muhammad Izzat Darwazah; and Isa al-Sifri, whose eulogy for Izz al-Din al-Qassam had a profound revolutionary significance.

This vigorous dynamism in the Palestinian cultural climate, which reached its zenith in the 1930s, took on various expressive forms as we have seen. But for various reasons, including the history and heritage of Arabic cultural production more broadly, pride of place was the preserve of poetry and popular poetry, and these held their ground as the main media through which Palestine's cultural effervescence was expressed. It was as if Arabic poetry in Palestine had tasked itself with the mission of mobilization through political proselytizing. As early as 1929, for instance, Ibrahim Tuqan deployed his verse to expose the role of the major landowners in the land question:

> They sold the country, greedy for gold
> > But it was their homeland that they sold
> They'd be forgiven had they been forced by hunger,
> > But by God, they have not thirsted a day, nor hungered

That same year, Tuqan wrote his epic on the Mandate government's orders to execute the three martyrs: Fuad Hijazi of Safad, and Muhamad Jamjoum and Ata al-Zir of al-Khalil. That poem became extremely famous, and came to be considered itself a part of the legacy left by the revolution that erupted half a decade later. This was also the case with the August 14, 1935 poem by Abd al-Rahim Mahmoud that was directed at Prince Sa'ud who visited Palestine on that day:

> Have you come to visit the Aqsa Mosque?
> Or have you come to bid farewell before it is lost?

Before Mahmoud would give his life at the Battle of al-Shajara (Tiberias district) in 1948, he played a prominent role alongside Abu Salma and Tuqan in laying the foundations for Palestinian resistance poetry that would become one of the pillars of steadfastness for the Palestinian masses under Israeli occupation.

It was poetry, both classical and popular/vernacular, that kept pace with the popular mass movement from the beginning of the 1930s, expressing the movement's eruption, its minutiae, and its richness. Abu Salma's poem narrating the 1936 Revolution, for example, daringly reveals the bitter disappointment felt toward Arab regimes' abandonment of the revolution:

> You who mourn the lands lost
> Rise up against oppression unashamed
> Liberate the land of its kings
> Liberate the land of its enslaved

He then goes on to remind us of the vernacular poet named Awad who, on the eve of his execution, wrote a powerful poem on the walls of his prison cell. The poem ends with the verses:

> I thought we had kings
> Behind whom men march in droves
> Shame on all kings
> If there are kings like these rogues
> By God, their crowns
> Are not fit to be on our shoes' soles
> We are the ones who protect
> The homeland and kiss its wounds[*]

The rage pouring out simultaneously against the trinity of enemies—Zionist colonization, the British Mandate, and Arab reactionary forces locally and regionally—grew in tandem with the deepening of the crisis. With the escalating acuteness of the contradictions and the eruption of armed intifadas, the countryside witnessed a development of a new consciousness through the interaction of its "intellectuals" with the cultural output of the cities. The vernacular poetry kept pace with verses such as:

> Oh people, what a blight
> A Zionist together with a Westerner [65]

And:

> The rifle has shown up, but the lion has not
>   Oh, barrel of the rifle, wet with his blood

---

[*] GK: Tawfiq Zayyad describes this poem as follows: "I do not know of a poetic work that can stand in the balance with this poem on the level of solidity, sacrifice, and courage." (Zayyad, "On literature" p.30).

And, similarly:

> The rifle in the hands of the salesman, I saw it
> I wish my heart would stop, why didn't I buy it?
> His rifle had rusted from stitting idle
> Rusted, and missing its owners

This even extended to wedding songs:

> The groom is one of us, those we fight had better watch out, we'll cut his mustache with a sword, shake the lance with the fine shaft
> and you brave men, where are you from?
> We are the youths of Palestine,
> Welcome, with pride and honor
> Oh father of the bride, don't you worry, we are the drinkers of blood
> In Bal'a and Wadi al-Tuffah* there was an attack and a battle of guns
> Oh fair and fine ones, ululate and celebrate
> On the day of the battle at Beit Imrin, you heard the gunfire of the *Martineh***
> Peek out at us from your balcony[66]

The incitement to rise up in revolt took on such power that, despite the heavy inheritance of quietist proverbs and sayings that had given submission the status of tradition, you could now hear a popular poem proclaiming:

---

* GK: Two villages near Nablus and Tulkarem in which Palestinians fought major battles against the British in 1936.
** Translator's note: Martini-Henry rifles, in service in the British imperial army until the end of WWI. With the outbreak of the 1936 revolution in Palestine, this outdated firearm was one of the most accessible to Palestinian peasants due to its proliferation in the region during and after the war. It was exclusively known in Arabic as al-Martineh.

You Arab, son of an impoverished mother
Sell your mother and buy a gun
A rifle is better than your mother
On revolution day, it will relieve you of your woes[67]

The accumulation and eruption of contradictions thus rendered the "rifle" the tool that could tear down that venerable wall of calls to quietism. All of a sudden, this "rifle" is able get to the heart of the matter, and revolution becomes a future more promising than all the maternal and familial warmth of the past. Over and above all of this, it was the feudal-clerical patriarchs who had been popularly unveiled as an ossified and impotent ally of this discredited past.

In the midst of these compounded and clashing contradictions—which were taking root more broadly and deeply, disproportionately affecting Arab peasants and workers while also weighing heavily on the petite and middle urban bourgeoisies as well as the middle peasants of the rural areas—the crisis deepened. It expressed itself from time to time in the form of armed outbreaks between 1928 and 1933.

For their part, the clerical Palestinian feudalists felt their interests threatened by the rising economic power of Jewish capital, allied as it was to the Mandatory power. But these interests were also facing a threat from the opposite direction: the impoverished Arab masses that did not know which way to turn. The Arab urban bourgeoisie was weak and incapable of leadership in this moment of unprecedently rapid economic change. A small segment of this bourgeoisie had positioned itself as a leech feeding off the scraps of Jewish industrial development. To the extent that this segment's subjective and material conditions surrounding it allowed, this segment charted a course completely opposite to the direction in which the Arab society was moving. Meanwhile, the educated scions of the wealthy urban and rural families stood out in their revolutionary agitation. They had returned from their universities to a society whose old modality of social relations they rejected, and which themselves were rapidly changing. Moreover, there was little room for these young intellectuals in the newer patterns of social relations, emerging as they were within the framework of the alliance between Zionism and imperialism.

So it was that the class struggle became so thoroughly intertwined with national demands and religious sentiment. With the intensification of the subjective and objective crisis experienced by Palestinian Arab society, this combination of forces exploded while still hostage to the feudal-clerical patriarchs. Given the social and economic repression of the Arab poor, both urban and rural, the patriotic movement had to adopt advanced forms that gave prominence to issues of class in its slogans and modes of struggle; in the face of the strong and ever-present alliance between the Zionist colonists and the British imperialists, it was impossible for the liberation movement to neglect the primary national dimension of the struggle; and in confronting the tremendous religious fervor evident in every manifestation of the Zionist colonization of Palestine, the backwards countryside could not but barricade itself behind politicized religiosity as a central facet of its battle against Zionist-imperial conquest.*

The feudal-clerical patriarchs advanced themselves as the leaders of the masses' movement, taking advantage of both the insipidness of the fledgling urban Arab bourgeoisie and the limited contradiction that had developed between these patriarchs and British imperialism, which focused its energies on its alliance with Zionism as the local

---

* In its commentary on the emergence of the Israeli Black Panther movement, the leftist Hebrew magazine *Matzpen* (Issue 58, April 1971) stated that "class contradictions in Israel can sometimes tend to find expression as sectarian contradictions. Class demands, even when translated into the language of sectarianism, have from the very beginning been at the core of Zionism." The correctness of this statement patently applies with even more intensity to the role played by religion in the resistance to Zionist conquest, given the latter's nature as simultaneously national and class oppression. One example that illustrates this is that "one of the results of Zionist colonialism... was that the mawlid al-nabawi [Prophet Muhammad's birthday] celebrations were transformed, under the aegis of the Mufti of Haifa and the poet Wadi' al-Bustani, into nationalist festivals. They were attended by Christian spiritual leaders and notables while none of their Jewish counterparts were invited. In this way, Muslim and Christian religious festivities became mass popular events taking the form of nationalist festivals in the cities of Palestine."

agent for its influence. The patriarchs' reputations as religious leaders also worked in their favor, as did the small size of the Arab proletariat and the weakness of its communist party, which was not only led by Jewish party members, but whose Arab members had been subjected to the violence and terrorism of the Arab feudalists since at least the late 1920s. It was against this multitextured backdrop of interwoven and complex contradictions that the 1936 Revolution took center stage in the history of Palestine.

THE REVOLUTION

Many a historian has rushed to claim a particular incident at a particular time and place as the cause for the 1936 Revolution's eruption. In Yehuda Bauer's estimation, for instance, the event that "is generally considered the start of the 1936 disturbances" took place on April 19, 1936 when "mobs of Arabs in Yafa attacked Jewish passersby."[68] According to Isa al-Sifri,[69] Saleh Mas'ud Abu Yaseen,[70] and Subhi Yasin,[71] the initial spark was an ambush carried out by a group of Arab militants (Yaseen states this was a Qassamist troop that included Farhan al-Sa'di and Mahmud al-Dirawi) who held up and robbed the Jewish and Arab passengers of fifteen vehicles traveling between Anabta and Nur Shams. According to al-Sifri, one of the militants gave a short speech to the passengers, the majority of whom were Arab, in which he proclaimed that the revolution had begun, and "we are taking your money so we can fight the enemy and defend you."[72] Dr. Abdul-Wahhab al-Kayyali[73] dates the spark of the revolution to an earlier event of February 1936 when a group of Arab workers surrounded the construction site of a school in Yafa that was being built by exclusively Jewish workers.

All sources concur, however, that the beginnings of the revolution lay in the intifada lead by Shaikh Izz al-Din al-Qassam. The Peel Commission Report,[74] which Bauer considers among the most reliable sources on the Palestine question, glides over particular trigger events by giving two principal causes for the eruption of the uprising: the Arabs' desire for national independence, and their antipathy and concern toward the establishment of a Jewish national home in Palestine. We can see that these two causes are in fact one and the same, despite their vague and nebulous phrasing. Lord Peel did, however, offer what he called "secondary factors" that helped spark the "disturbances," namely: (1) the growth of Arab national sentiment beyond Palestine; (2) the increasing rate of Jewish immigration since 1933; (3) the opportunity afforded to Jews to influence British public opinion; (4) Arab distrust of the British government's fidelity; (5) Arab anxiety over continued Jewish land purchases; and (6) the lack of clarity regarding the British Mandate government's ultimate objectives.

We can get a sense of how the leaders of the Palestinian patriotic movement understood the causes of the uprising from the three main slogans that summed up their demands: (1) the immediate halt to Jewish immigration; (2) prohibition on the transfer of title to land from Arab landholders to Jewish buyers; and (3) the establishment of a democratic government in which Arabs would hold a majority position given their greater numbers among the population.[75] These slogans, and the indeterminate ways in which they were spread and reiterated, were incapable of expressing the reality of the situation, their effectiveness largely restricted to their role in maintaining the feudalists' hegemony over the national movement.

The real causes of the revolution's outbreak were, as discussed above, that the intensity of the contradictions imbricated in society's transition from the Arab feudal-clerical agrarian economy to a Jewish bourgeois industrial (western) economy had reached a peak. Furthermore, as we've also already seen, the mid-1930s was when the process of deepening and entrenching the colonial condition reached its peak through the transition from British Mandate rule to Zionist settler colonialism. The leaders of the Palestinian patriotic movement were thus obliged to take up the armed form of struggle because they could not otherwise have remained enthroned as the legitimate leadership when the contradictions had reached the point of decisive confrontation. A number of different, and contradictory, factors drove the leadership at the time to adopt the armed struggle. First among these was the Qassamist movement. Second were the chain of failures with which this leadership was blessed while it sat, ossified, at the movement's head. Indeed, this leadership was unable to wrest even the tiniest partial concessions of the kind colonizers are often eager to concede for the purpose of venting the natives' resentment (the British would later come to appreciate the opportunities that such a tactic could offer, immunized against any feeling of urgency to appease Arab notables by the ready presence of more competent Zionist collaborators). The third factor was that of colonial violence, both in the form of Jewish violence (the armed garrisons, the slogan of exclusive Jewish labor, and so on) and that of the British Mandate regime (the brutality with which the British repressed the 1929 uprising, etc.).

Any discussion of the 1936–1939 Revolution requires an appreciation of the particular place held by Shaikh Izz al-Din al-Qassam. Despite the volume of writing on al-Qassam, we can confidently say that this unique figure remains, and may likely remain, largely unknown; most of what has been written has only scratched the surface. This superficiality of the literature on al-Qassam has allowed several Jewish historians to characterize him as a "fanatical dervish," while Western historians have largely ignored him altogether. The underestimation of the Qassamist movement's importance in the literature is directly attributable to this literature's authors' deficient understanding of the dialectical relationship between religion and nationalist tendencies in the world's underdeveloped societies. Opinions may differ on al-Qassam as a thinker, but there can be no doubt whatsoever that the Qassamist movement was a turning point in its adoption of an advanced form of struggle. By doing so, the Qassamists put the fragmented and scattered traditional Palestinian leaders to the test, a test they could no longer avoid.

Al-Qassam himself formed a remarkable symbolic knot joining together many of the interwoven factors that weave into the complex tapestry we simplify as "the Palestinian cause." Born in Jableh (Latakia district) in 1871, his "Syrianness" represented the Arab national dimension of the battle. As a graduate of al-Azhar, his Azharism represented the religio-patriotic dimension that the Cairene university and mosque stood for earlier in the century. Having taken an active role in the armed resistance against the French in 1919–20, for which he was sentenced to death, his association with militant struggle represented the unity of Arab struggle.

Al-Qassam came to Haifa with the Shaikh Ali Hajj 'Ubaid and the Egyptian Sheikh Muhammad al-Hanafi in 1921, and immediately began setting up secret groups. Among his most remarkable traits were his advanced organizational capacity and his ironclad patience. In 1929, he refused to prematurely bring his organized network of armed militants into the open. And though this restraint caused a split in his organization, it held together and managed to steer clear of British detection. According to one well-known Qassamist,[76] al-Qassam devised his strategy as one that would unfold in four stages: first, psychological preparation and spreading revolutionary spirit; second, the establishment of secret groups; third, the formation of committees, each with a particular task such as collecting donations, purchasing arms, military training, security and espionage, propaganda and information, and political communications; fourth, armed revolt.

Most of those well-informed about al-Qassam confirm that the purpose of his infamous last foray to the hills of Ya'bad with twenty-five of his men on the night of November 12, 1935 was not to declare an armed uprising, but to mobilize support for one. It was an unexpected clash that led to his whereabouts that night ever being known. Despite the mettlesome fight al-Qassam and his men put up, the British troops they encountered easily overpowered them. It seems that when Sheikh al-Qassam realized he and his comrades would not be able to continue to mobilize for the revolution, he raised a new slogan: "die in battle as martyrs." We would do justice to al-Qassam to take this last slogan as expressing of a kind of Guevara-esque heroism. The few first-person testimonies of al-Qassam that we do have, however, suggest that he appreciated the significance of the role he himself played as the explosive force fueling a forward revolutionary *foco*. The effect was immediate: masses of people came to walk in the ten-kilometer burial procession to the village of Yajur. What is most significant about this moment is that it exposed the traditional leaders to the challenge of everything Sheikh al-Qassam represented, a challenge that leadership felt just as acutely as the British Mandate authorities.

According to one Qassamist, al-Qassam had delivered a message through Musa al-Azrawi to the Mufti, Hajj Amin al-Husseini. In it, the Sheikh asked the Mufti to coordinate the declaration of a countrywide revolt. Al-Husseini refused, claiming the conditions were not yet ripe for such action.[77]

The only people who marched in al-Qassam's funeral procession were the poor. The leaders' reaction, by contrast, was one of indifference. They would soon come to regret this; al-Qassam's martyrdom was a momentous event they could not simply bypass by looking the other way. The clearest proof of this is that representatives of all five Palestinian political parties delivered a memorandum to the British High Commissioner barely six days after the killing of al-Qassam. The memorandum is a rare gem of these leaders' flagrant impudence; in it, they admit that "if they do not receive a generally satisfactory answer to this memorandum, they would lose all the influence they held over their followers. Irresponsibly extremist views would then come to hold sway, and the situation would deteriorate rapidly as a result."[78]

Evidently, these leaders aimed to use the Qassam phenomenon to achieve a solid step backward. But through the form of resistance he had introduced, al-Qassam had stolidly blocked their retreat. Indeed, this is how we can make sense of the dramatic change of heart evidenced by these leaders between between al-Qassam's funeral procession and the fortieth day commemoration of his martyrdom. It took those forty days for them to realize that failure to crest the tidal wave set in motion by al-Qassam would lead to their being swallowed by the sea of popular frustration. So it was that they went from flapping about at the time of his funeral, to racing to attend every event and give every speech at the fortieth day commemoration events. It is also evident that Hajj Amin al-Husseini would continue to feel the weight of his own inadequacy; the official organ of Husseini's Arab Higher Committee (the newspaper *Filastin*) consistently worked to imply that the Qassamist movement was a part of the broader movement headed by the Mufti, claiming the al-Qassam and al-Husseini were "personal friends."79

As for the British, their version of the story is contained in the report they submitted to the League of Nations in Geneva on the events of 1935, and in which they stated that

> rumors of the formation of terrorist bands, inspired by political and religious motives, had been rife for some time, and on November 7 a police sergeant, following up a case of theft in the hills of Nazareth sub-district, was shot dead by unknown persons. This event quickly led up to the discovery of the existence in that neighborhood of an armed band under the leadership of Sheikh Izzed Din al-Qassam [*sic*], a political refugee from Syria, possessing no little reputation as a man of religion, and already strongly suspected of being concerned in terroristic acts a few years ago. . . . The funeral of Sheikh Izzed Din at Haifa was attended by a very large concourse, and in spite of the efforts of leading Muslims there to maintain order a certain amount of demonstration and stone-throwing occurred. The death of Sheikh Izzed Din sent a strong wave of sentiment through political and other circles in the country, and the Arabic press united to pay him the tributes of a martyr in articles charged with patriotic emotion.80

For their part, the British felt the acuteness of the challenge posed by al-Qassam's martyrdom, and they too tried to turn back the clock. In a memorandum to the British colonial secretary, the High Commissioner expressed that failure to grant the Arab leaders' demands would result in them "losing what influence they hold, and the possibility of pacifying the present situation by the suggested moderate means would vanish."[81]

It was turning back the clock that would prove impossible. Al-Qassam's movement was the expression of the natural form that would be able to decisively remedy the swelling contradiction. It did not take long before different committees and formations began to proliferate. The traditional leaders now had to choose between standing in the way of the rising tide of the popular will to fight, or to try and somehow absorb the flood by positioning themselves as its ossified bowsprits.

Though the British were quick to act, their offers to set up a legislative assembly and impose restrictions on land sales had come too late. The Zionist movement, which had begun making its own agenda forcefully known at this time, played a significant part in undermining the effectiveness of the British offer. Even so, the Palestinian leadership had yet to make a clear choice, with a vacillation so unmistakable we can only be left stupefied. Up until at least April 1936, the representatives of the Palestinian political parties were still considering forming a delegation that would travel to London to offer their point of view to the British government. The uprising erupted before that leadership had worked out a course of action. At the time of the February 1936 Yafa riot, the leaders were still thinking they could win some partial concessions from the British through negotiation. The events that followed would be a rude awakening: the recollections of those who were close to the center of events at the time all confirm that the eruption of militant violence and civil disobedience was spontaneous, and with the exception of particular actions by the remaining Qassamists, the initial uprising was a spontaneous expression of the acuteness of the contradiction. Even when the general strike was announced on the nineteenth of that same month, the national movement leadership lagged behind, though it finally managed to jump onto the train just as it was leaving the station. We have already discussed the socio-political situation in Palestine to explain why the leadership managed to ultimately impose its dominance on the nationalist movement.

From an organizational standpoint, the Palestinian nationalist movement was effectively comprised of political parties that were by and large the remaining sediments of the movements that had formed against the Ottoman Empire in the early 1900s. On the one hand, this meant that these formations, unlike their counterparts in Egypt, had little to no experience sustaining an independence struggle. What it also meant was that these were effectively vacuous formations, lacking any specific principles per se. Rather, they were groupings headed by gangs of notables that depended on the loyalties those notables could garner on the basis of their status-based influence as clerics, landowners, or clan patriarchs. In no way can we think of them as political factions with organized cadre and popular support bases. With the important exception of al-Qassam himself (and, of course, the communists), not one of the leaders of the Palestinian national movement at this time was armed with a strategic organizational mind. Though he possessed rare administrative capabilities, Hajj Amin al-Husseini was a far cry from the kind of leader who could conceive and carry out a sustained organized struggle. The burden of organizational work remained mostly confined to individuals at the level of subcommittees and mid-level cadre who could not codify or institutionalize their talents.

After the dissolution of the Arab Executive Committee in August 1934, six formations emerged that comprised the Palestinian national movement on the eve of the revolution:

> 1) the Palestinian Arab Party (formed in May 1935) was led by Jamal al-Husseini. For the most part, it pushed the Mufti's agenda and represented the major feudalists and urban merchants;

2) the National Defense Party (formed in December 1934) was led by Ragheb al-Nashashibi. It represented the emergent urban bourgeoisie and high-wage professionals;

3) the Independence Party (formed in 1932) was led by Awni Abd al-Hadi. It brought together the intellectuals, middle bourgeoisie, and some parts of the petite bourgeoisie. This enabled its left wing to play a special role within it;

4) the Reform Party (formed in August 1935) was led by Dr. Hussein al-Khalidi, and represented a number of intellectuals;

5) the National Bloc led by Abd al-Latif Salah;

6) the Palestine Youth Party led by Ya'qub al-Ghusain.

This political pluralism existed only at the surface level and was not a clear and definite expression of the country's class configuration. The vast majority of the masses were not represented by any of the formations (according to Neville Barbour, 90% of the revolutionaries were peasants who considered themselves volunteers). The representativeness of the political parties is made all the more clear when we consider the class structure of Palestine: in 1931, 59% of the Arab population (and 19.1% of the Jewish population) were peasants; 12.9% of the Arab population (30.6% of the Jewish population) worked in construction, manufacture, or mining; 6% of the Arab population worked in transportation, 8% in commerce, 1.3% in administration, and so on.[82] What this means is that the overwhelming majority of the population was not represented by these parties. Though the parties did represent the feudalists, clerics, urban compradors, and certain sectors of the intelligentsia, they were always subject to the leadership of the Mufti and his class—that class that represented clerical feudalism, and that was more patriotic than the leadership representing the urban bourgeoisie. For its part, the urban bourgeoisie was represented by the *effendiyya* at a time in which the former were increasingly directing their investments toward industry (a trend that would become all the more evident after the defeat of the 1936–1939 Revolution).

For their part, the petite bourgeoisie (small merchants, shopkeepers, teachers, employees, and craftspeople) were generally leaderless. As a class, they remained without political influence or importance under the rule of the Ottomans, who relied on the *effendiyya* class for the purposes of local government due to its having developed in close association with the feudal aristocracy. The labor movement, despite its weakness and the recentness of its emergence, was trammeled by the brutal repression of the Mandate authorities, the crushing competition of the Jewish proletariat and bourgeoisie, and oppression by leadership of the Arab patriotic movement.

In the leadup to the formation of the Mufti-led Arab Higher Committee on April 25, 1936, Jamal al-Husseini (leader of the Arab Party) had expressed his exasperation with the growing popular feeling that the English were the real enemy. The National Defense Party, which primarily represented the emergent urban comprador class, was in no way disposed toward an open clash with the British. Only two days prior, on April 23, Chairman Chaim Weizmann of the World Zionist Organization gave a speech in Tel Aviv in which he described the intensifying Arab–Zionist conflict as one between agents of destruction and agents of construction. This powerful description cast the Zionist forces in their role as an instrument of colonialism on the eve of battle. This was how the different forces positioned themselves on each side of the battlefield in the direct lead up to the revolution!

The revolt in the countryside took the form of civil disobedience and armed insurrection. Hundreds of armed militants joined the bands that began to proliferate in the highlands. The tax strike had been decided and declared on May 7, 1936 by around 150 delegates representing the Arabs of Palestine at a conference held at the Rawdat al-Ma'arif al-Wataniyah college in Jerusalem. A glance at the names of those delegates, as compiled by Isa al-Sifri,[83] shows that it was at this particular conference that the leadership of the popular movement was handed to an insipid alliance of feudal-religious leaders, urban commercial bourgeois figures, and a narrow set of intellectuals. The resolution passed at the conference was brief, but offered a very clear expression of the limits to how far such a leadership was prepared to go: "The congregants have unanimously decided to call a tax strike beginning on May 15 of this year so long as the British government does not make a fundamental change to its policies through which to show the intention of stopping Jewish immigration."

In their response to the movement of civil disobedience and armed insurrection, British authorities directed their attacks at two main bodies: the organizational cadre that was largely more revolutionary than the leadership, and the impoverished masses participating in the uprising, which had nothing protecting them except the weapons they bore. This helps explain why the British only arrested two of the top leaders of the uprising, Awni Abd al-Hadi and Muhammad Izzat Darwazah, the two men who had relatively high organizational skills among that echelon of leaders. None of the others were subjected to the kind of arrest or harassment that would put a stop to their efforts. A further illustration is that on May 23, the British arrested sixty-one of the mid-level cadre leading the tax strike at the same time that those same British authorities granted travel permits to four of the upper echelon leaders (Jamal al-Husseini, Shibli al-Jamal, Abd al-Latif Salah, and Dr. Izzat Tannus) for the purpose of traveling to London to meet with the colonial secretary on June 12. Rather than being unusual, such incidents would be repeated *ad nauseum* in the months and years to follow. Indeed, the High Commissioner remarked with great satisfaction that "Friday sermons have been marked by a degree of moderation that far exceeds what I would have expected at a time when emotions are so charged. This is primarily thanks to the Mufti."[84]

The movement leadership's positioning was clear from the outset: it saw the mass popular uprising as a mere tool with which to apply pressure on the British colonial authorities to advance the leaders' own class interests. The British were profoundly aware of this, and acted accordingly. Despite this, the British did not deign to go to any extra lengths to make any of the concessions that class sought; London dug its heels, insistent upon fulfilling its commitment to hand over the mantle of the colonizer to the Zionist movement. To the contrary, the years of the revolution (1936–39) were a period in which British colonialism threw its weight behind the goal of solidifying the Zionist presence and standing it on its feet, as we will see further on. The British employed two means to bring about this goal: first by striking at the impoverished peasant revolutionaries with unparalleled violence, and second by using their extensive influence with the Arab regimes that ultimately played a major role in pacifying the revolt.

With regards the first of these means (violent repression), the British Emergency Regulations performed their purpose with great effectiveness. Al-Sifri gives a list of sentences issued at the time to exemplify the repressiveness of the regulations: "Six-year prison sentence for possession of a firearm; twelve years for possession of a bomb; five years hard labor for possession of twelve rounds of ammunition; eight months for giving a group of British soldiers wrong directions; nine years for the possession of small explosives; five years for attempting to buy ammunition from soldiers; two weeks for possession of a stick; etc."[85] According to a British estimate reported to the League of Nations, the number of Arab casualties over the course of the 1936 Revolution was around one thousand killed, not counting those injured, missing, or imprisoned. The British also adopted a policy of widescale home demolition. On June 18, 1936, British authorities blew up and destroyed a large part of the city of Yafa, with an estimated 220 homes demolished and around 6,000 people forced out of their homes. In addition to this, in the suburbs surrounding Yafa they destroyed 100 huts in al-Jabaliyah, 300 in Abu Kabir, 250 in al-Shaikh

Murad, and 75 in 'Arab al-Dawudi. It is evident that the inhabitants of the Yafa neighborhoods and outskirts whose homes were destroyed were poor peasants who had moved to the towns from the countryside. As for the villages, al-Sifri counted 143 homes razed under pretexts directly related to the revolution.[86] These homes belonged to poorer peasants, some medium peasants, and a very small number of feudal landowning families.

With regards the second of the British strategies of pacification (pressure on Arab regimes), Prince Abdullah of Transjordan and Nuri al-Sa'id of Iraq began their efforts as British intermediaries with the Arab Higher Committee. Despite the willingness of the Palestinian leaders to comply, the mediation, which took place in August 1936, failed because the mass movement was not yet ready or willing to be domesticated. The negotiations had a detrimental effect on the revolution, as they left the impression that the contradiction was resolvable through some kind of negotiated settlement. Indeed, this initially failed negotiation initiative would achieve a complete success in October of that same year, just six weeks later!

These contacts were not, however, the only form assumed by the dialectic of relations between Palestine and the neighboring Arab countries. That dialectic was more complex, reflecting the compounded contradictions as a whole. We have already noted what al-Qassam represented in this context. That aspect of the Qassamist phenomenon continued; large numbers of Arab fighters flocked to Palestine. Among these were figures such as Sa'id al-'As (martyred in October 1936), Sheikh Muhammad al-Ashmar, and many others. The fighters crossing into Palestine to join the struggle also included a number of patriot adventurers who were trained military officers. The most notorious of these was Fawzi al-Qawuqji, who, shortly after entering Palestine with his small band of fighters, declared himself the general commander of the revolution. Though these officers augmented and improved the revolutionaries' tactics, the brunt of the revolutionary burden in the countryside and the guerrilla action in the cities remained primarily on the shoulders of the dispossessed peasants. It was actually the "officers" who emerged from the ranks of these peasants that played the leading role throughout. Despite being ostensibly under the leadership of the Mufti, it was these peasant officers who represent the epic heroism of the masses in this revolution.

British officials stationed in Palestine did not fully agree with London's reckless backing of the Zionist movement. Their preference was to chart a course that would foster relations with the Arab class leadership whose interests did not intersect with those of the revolution. Despite this, imperial strategy seems to have settled with some finality on a position that gave priority to the "importance of the organic link between the safety of British interests and the success of Zionism in Palestine."[87] It thus decided to buttress British military power in Palestine and to intensify its measures of violent repression.

The British decision to put its military weight at the service of Zionist goals shook the leadership of the Palestinian patriotic movement. Overtaken by fear, these leaders lost their bearings; Hajj Amin al-Husseini, Ragheb Nashashibi, and Awni Abd al-Hadi rushed to meet with the British High Commissioner. The reports sent by the latter to his superiors suggest that the Palestinian notables made a big show of suggesting that they were prepared to put an end to the revolution "if the Arab kings asked them to do so." These same notables, however, would never dare admit to the masses that they were behind such a crooked scheme. In fact, they repeatedly denied it. It was in the wake of this meeting that London sent around 20,000 soldiers to Palestine. On September 30, 1936, with these troops all in place, the Mandate government instituted martial law, redoubling its unyielding policy of violent pacification. The autumn months of 1936 thus witnessed the most violent of battles. These were practically the last set of battles to encompass most of the geographical landmass of Palestine at the time.

On October 11, 1936, the Arab Higher Committee distributed a communiqué calling for the end of the general strike and, by extension, the revolution. It stated:

Whereas submission to the will of their Majesties and Highnesses, the Arab kings, and compliance with their wishes is one of our inherited Arab traditions; and given that the Arab [Higher] Committee firmly believes that their Majesties and Highnesses would not command their sons to take any but the actions that would be in the people's interests and with the purpose of protecting their rights; the Arab Higher Committee has, in obedience to the will of their Majesties and Highnesses, the Kings and Princes, and stemming from its belief in the great benefit that will result from their mediation and support, calls on the noble Arab people to end the strike and strife, pursuant to these noble orders, who have no object but the interests of the Arabs.[88]

Exactly one month later, on November 11, the "General Command of the Arab Revolution in Southern Syria-Palestine" issued a communiqué signed by Fawz al-Din al-Qawuqji, and which called for "a halt to all acts of violence, and refrain from any provocation that could disrupt the negotiations, about which the Arab nation is optimistic, and through which it aims to obtain its fullest rights."[89] Ten days later, the same leadership body issued another statement announcing "withdrawal from the battlefield, reliant on the guarantees of the Arab kings and princes, and in the interests of the negotiations."[90] According to Jamil al-Shuqairi, "thus, following the orders of the kings and princes, the strike was called off, and revolutionary action came to a halt within two hours of the communiqué's release."[91]

Despite Britain challenging the Palestinian leaders on precisely the same issue over which they had misled the masses, namely the issue of Jewish immigration to Palestine, and despite these leaders' decision to boycott the Palestine Royal Commission headed by Lord Peele, the Arab kings and princes obliged these leaders to obediently comply for the second time in three months. Kings Abd al-Aziz Al Saud of

Saudi Arabia and Ghazi of Iraq wrote letters to Hajj Amin al-Husseini stating that "... in view of our confidence in the good intentions of the British government to do justice by the Arabs, it is our opinion that your interest requires that you meet with the Royal Commission." This seemingly tangential incident tore apart the alliance leading the patriotic movement: the forces to the right of Hajj Amin al-Husseini, led by the Defense Party, hastened to oppose any boycott of the Peel Commission. The Defense Party, which predominantly represented the interests of the urban *effendiyya*, offered a series of indications that it would accept any settlement the British would propose. The Party's leadership justified itself on the basis of the discontent expressed by the major urban merchants as a result of the general strike, and the harm caused to the interests of the urban bourgeoisie, which relied on the strong economic relations most clearly manifested in this bourgeoisie's role as licensed agents for British, and in some cases Jewish, industry.

The Arab regimes, especially that of Transjordan, strongly supported this right-wing position. For their part, Hajj Amin al-Husseini and the currents he represented had no incentive to chart a more left leaning course, and instead embarked on an attempt to eliminate the more progressive currents. The Mufti's position thus took on a more reluctant, dithering path that made it all the more apparent that the revolution would not make even the slightest advance with him at its helm. What is more, the revolution's retreat no longer really served his interests. When the British believed the moment was ripe to politically eliminate the Mufti in the period of quiet that came in the wake of the general strike's end, they were dismayed to realize that they had miscalculated: the currents to the right of the Mufti were still far too weak to assert control of the situation. The British High Commissioner, Arthur Wauchope, guilefully continued to appreciate the crucial role the Mufti could play while sandwiched between the Defense Party to his right, and the Independence Party (the left wing of his coalition) and the movements of young intellectuals to his left. Wauchope appreciated the extent to which Britain could benefit from the wide gulf separating the "rugged solidity of the villagers who resisted us for six months on meager pay, which they did not make up for with plunder" and the "weakness and absence of any great leadership qualities among the ten members of the (Arab Higher) Committee."[92]

The High Commissioner's assessment of the limited role the Mufti's right wing could play was proven correct when the Defense Party failed to take a clear stance against the Peel Commission Report when it was issued on July 7, 1937, proposing the partition of Palestine and the establishment of a Jewish state. It also became clear, at the same moment, that the High Commissioner's concerns that the currents to the left of the Mufti could pressure him to veer off the moderate path were well founded. That pressure, however, did not come from the quarters Wauchope expected, but from the mid-level cadre who continued to meet through their local committees to represent the daily concerns of the landless peasants and unemployed workers of the cities and the villages.

So it was that the Mufti had no choice but to retreat forward. He sidestepped arrest by taking asylum in the Haram al-Sharif, but the course of events forced him to take a position that would have been unimaginable just a year before: in September 1937, four armed guerrillas shot and killed Lewis Andrews, District Commissioner of the Galilee region, as he was leaving the Anglican Church in Nazareth. "Andrews was the only official who administered the Mandate in a way that the Zionists would have considered correct, failing to gain the Arab peasants' trust." The Arabs regarded him as a friend of the Jews, whose mission was to facilitate the transfer of the Galilee to the Jewish state proposed by the partition plan. That is why the Arab peasants detested him, accusing him of facilitating the Zionist acquisition of the lands of the Hula valley. The guerrillas who assassinated him are thought to have been members of a secret Qassamist cell.[93]

Although the Arab Higher Committee immediately condemned the assassination, they found themselves in a position similar to the one they faced with the martyrdom of al-Qassam: they were not in control of those they ostensibly led. To remain at the helm of the national movement, they needed to once again race toward the wave of popular sentiment and mount it. It was April 1936 all over again. But this time, the popular fervor for revolution was far fiercer. This was not only due to the experience of revolution gained over the preceding year: the fundamental contradiction had become glaringly clear; it was right before their eyes. This next stage of the revolution undoubtedly saw an overwhelming, not to say total, shift of focus toward the British occupation, and away from Zionist colonization. The intensification of the contradiction meant the battle lines were more clearly drawn, and more deeply entrenched: the peasants took almost complete control over the revolution, the urban bourgeoisie retreated somewhat, the upper echelons of the peasantry hesitantly supported the revolutionaries, and the Zionist forces effectively went on the offensive.

Two aspects of this stage of the revolution are particularly salient and warrant some analysis. The first is that "the Arabs contacted the Jews to propose a deal to be arrived at on the basis of completely severing all ties with Britain, but the Jews immediately rejected the proposal because they consider their relations with Britain to be of fundamental importance."[94] In this period, a growing number of Jewish colonists joined the police force. This number had grown from 365 police personnel in 1935 to 682 in 1936. At the end of 1936, the government announced that it would induct 1,240 more Jewish colonists into the police force where they would be equipped with military grade rifles, and this number went up to 2,863 just one month later.[95] Several British officers distinguished themselves by leading Jewish forces in attacks on Arab villages. The second important aspect of this stage of the revolution was that as the leadership came to be based outside of Palestine, in Damascus, the leadership on the ground was increasingly composed of local commanders hailing from poor peasant families, which was in stark contrast to the previous stages of the revolt. The close social bonds between these commanders and the peasantry go a long way in helping to explain the increased collective capacities of the revolutionaries at this stage. It was in this period, for example, that future general commander of the revolution, Abd al-Rahim al-Hajj Muhammad, became prominent on a national scale. The Communists say they were in contact with him and provided him with intelligence.[96] The potential for such a development to have proved a real historic turning point in the revolution was undercut by two main factors. First, the weakness of the "Left" in both its relative and actual formations; second, the necessity that local commanders maintain some degree of organizational ties to the Central Committee of Jihad in Damascus, not just because of a certain tradition of loyalty, but because the local commanders relied to some extent on the material support coming from Damascus.

At no point in the entire history of the Palestinian struggle was the armed popular revolution as close to victory as it was in those months stretching from the end of 1937 to the beginning of 1939. The British military's hold over Palestine was severely weakened, and the colonizer's prestige had plummeted to new depths of ignominy. The high esteem with which the masses held up the revolution became the primary force across the country. As a result, British decision makers hardened in their conviction that they had to depend on Zionist military force if Britain wanted long term control over the situation. The Zionists had, after all, created conditions unique among Britain's colonies by offering itself as a local force sharing common cause with British colonial objectives, fully charged and mobilized against the indigenous population.

It was also during this period that Britain began to grow alarmed by the prospect of having to move part of its military force to face the growing threat of war in Europe. In light of this, the British quickly moved toward "the rapid formation of a Jewish volunteer defense force to supplement the existing force that numbered 6,500 armed men."[97] The Mandate government had already made significant strides in line with the policy of reliance on the local Zionist force, devolving an expanding ambit of tasks of repression to these local allies. At the same time, the British maintained its contact with the leadership of the classes headed by the Mufti. In this particular context, and in this particular period, the British played a crucial role in propping up the Mufti as the uncontested representative of Palestine's Arabs. Those figures to the right of the Mufti who the British had identified as backup substitutes had practically lost all credibility. Anything that would detract from the Mufti as sole leader would effectively, in the words of the High Commissioner, "leave no one to represent the Arabs except the revolt's commanders in the hills."[98] Among other factors, this was a key reason that Hajj Amin al-Husseini was kept at the apex of the Palestinian national movement despite having dramatically fled his hiding place in the Aqsa Mosque and quartered himself in Damascus from late October 1937.

British repression escalated with unexpected intensity. The growing number of police raids, mass arrests, and executions exhausted the revolution, but did not put an end to it. The British came to realize that the revolution—in its essence and its substance as well as in terms of its local leadership—was a peasant revolt. This led the British to attempt to sow divisions in society by giving preferential treatment to urbanites. The revolutionary spirit that had taken hold throughout Palestinian society led to the mass adoption of peasant headdress (the *kufiyah* and *'iqal*) in the cities so that villagers visiting the city would be harder to single out for repression by the authorities. As the situation developed, the revolutionaries forbade all from carrying their identity cards with them to further hinder the authorities' ability to distinguish between urbanites and peasants.

These stories of the period clearly indicate the nature of the revolt and its widespread popular influence. The countryside was by and large the revolution's womb. Even the temporary British miliary occupations of several towns in 1938 were carried out as reprisals for Arab guerrilla operations in those towns that were carried out by peasant guerrillas hailing from the countryside.* This suggests that it was the peasants

---

* GK: In May 1938, the rebels occupied Hebron after they had already occupied the old port of Jerusalem. On September 9, they occupied Beersheba and released prisoners. On October 5, they occupied Tiberias; in early August parts of Nablus, etc.

and villagers who paid the highest price; in 1938, the British sentenced numerous peasants to death for the mere possession of weapons. A quick rundown of the names of those sent to the prisons and gallows reveals that the vast majority were poorer peasants. In one telling instance "the entire population of the village of 'Ain el-Karem, numbering 3,000 people, were sentenced to a ten-kilometer march each day to report to the nearest police station."[99] In that same period, the British occupiers sentenced about 2,000 Palestinians to very long prison terms, demolished over 5,000 homes, and hanged 148 people at the infamous Akka prison. The number of those detained or serving prison terms of any length during this period was around 50,000 people.[100]

In an attempt to win itself some time, the British abandoned the Peel Commission's partition proposal in November 1938. A few months later, in February 1939, it held the roundtable talks in London. These were effectively a visible version of those same shady dealings that had been taking place between the British and the formal leadership of the revolution in secret throughout the period of the uprising. The British, after all, knew that the leadership was desperate to submit to a deal at any time. Jamal al-Husseini, of course, did not go to the London talks alone, he was accompanied by representatives of the Arab countries considered "independent" at the time. So it was that the Arab regimes, still under the colonizer's yoke themselves, imposed their will for a second time in under two years upon the Arabs of Palestine through the latent and potential common interests of all those who sat around the roundtable in London.

Speeches were delivered in London by Jamal al-Husseini, Prince Faisal (representing Saudi Arabia), Prince Hussein (representing Yemen), Ali Maher (representing Egypt), and Nuri al-Sa'id (representing Iraq), the latter declaring that he spoke "as a close friend of Great Britain who does not want to say a single word that might hurt the feelings of any Briton because the friendship he felt for them stemmed from the bottom of his heart."[101] The only thing confirmed by the speeches overall was that the British strategy toward the Palestinian leadership—quietly fostered for over a decade—had succeeded; Britain had not done away with the line of contact it kept with that leadership, keeping the Palestinian leaders at arm's reach. The British were confident that Iraq and Saudi Arabia were "prepared to exert their influence on Palestinian leaders to put an end to the revolt and create the conditions that would ensure the success of the conference."

But the revolution had not quieted down. Official figures for February 1939 alone said as much: 110 killed and 112 injured in twelve battles against the British; 39 villages subjected to police and military searches; curfew imposed on three cities on three separate occasions; the arrest of 200 villagers; arson attacks on five government buildings; ten Arabs executed for possession of firearms; attacks on ten Jewish colonies; one attack on a petroleum pipeline; another on the Haifa–Lydd railway; and the establishment of a search post in the Aqsa Mosque. The government's figures, as presented by the British Colonial Secretary, indicated that "between December 20 and February 20 [i.e., in a two-month period], there had been 348 assassination attempts, 140 acts of sabotage, 190 kidnappings, 23 robberies, 9 landmines had been set off and 32 explosives detonated, the British forces had lost 18 soldiers with another 39 injured, while the civilian population had experienced 83 killings and 124 injuries. The figures do not include casualties among the revolutionaries."[102]

This was the situation until the British entry into World War II in September 1939. The losses suffered by the Arabs of Palestine over the course of this period were devastating. The leadership, and the whole spirit of defeatist compromise that it nurtured, lay outside the country. The emerging local commanders had fallen, one after the other, on the fields of battle. Violent British repression had reached its apex, and Zionist violence had been on the rise since mid-1937. There can be no doubt that these processes, and the dogged British military fixation on the Palestinian theater, exhausted the revolutionaries. In the context of this exhaustion, the dithering of the leadership brought the revolutionaries to a point where they could no longer be certain who they were fighting and why. At one moment, the leadership would speak of a tradition of friendship and common cause with Britain, at another the leaders would express their acceptance of Jewish self-administration in their settlements. The vacillation and impotence of the leadership, and its inability to formulate a coherent objective for the struggle, definitely aggravated the revolutionaries' exhaustion, but this should not lead us to brush the objective conditions aside. The British committed two divisions to quelling the uprising, together with aerial and police power, as well as the capabilities of the Transjordan Frontier Force. Also joining the fray against the revolutionaries were the 6,000 troops of the Jewish auxiliary forces. Indeed, the Peel Commission had admitted that British security expenditure in Palestine had risen from £862,000 in 1935 to £2,223,000 in 1936. This campaign of violent terrorism, especially the efforts made to sever the revolutionaries from their villages, was the primary factor in sapping the revolution's energy.

The killing of Abd al-Rahim al-Hajj Muhammad in March 1939 came as a crushing blow; the revolution had lost one of its most popular, revolutionary, courageous, wise, and sincere commanders. In the wake of his martyrdom, the network of local commanders began to unravel, many of them leaving the battlefield altogether. The world was closing in on the revolutionaries, and the warming of ties between the British and the French on the eve of the world war was yet another step in the isolation of the revolution. Worn out by hunger in the wilderness, Arif Abd al-Razeq and some of his troop's members surrendered to French forces. At around the same time, Transjordanian forces arrested Yusuf Abu Durrah and handed him over to the British who executed him. The collective punishment of villagers led them to fear British reprisal for supporting the guerrillas by, for example, providing them food and ammunition. The problems the revolution had with regards its own leadership meant that the minimum level of organization needed to tackle such challenges was no longer in place.

In its analysis at the time, the Communist Party attributed the failure of the revolution to five principal factors: the absence of a revolutionary leadership; the individualism and opportunism of the revolt's leaders; the absence of a central military command for the armed revolutionary forces; the weakness of the Palestine Communist Party; and the unfavorable global context.[103] This is a correct analysis, overall, but what must also be added is that the Communist Party chose Hajj Amin al-Husseini as its primary ally among the revolutionary leadership, considering him as "belonging to the most radical wing of the national movement in its hostility to colonialism," and branding his enemies within the movement as "traitorous feudalists."[104] It should also be noted, in this context, that the Mufti and his coterie never ceased to do what they could to eliminate leftists who tried to organize the workers. Over and above its weakness, the communist Left was unable to develop any base among the peasantry. Its main areas of operation were particular cities, and it had failed to Arabize itself in line with the recommendations of the seventh congress of the Comintern. Moreover, not only did the Party remain shortsighted with regards to the question of pan-Arab unity, it failed to grasp the bonds of struggle that transcended the borders between Arab societies, which had important ramifications at the level of revolutionary organizing.

It appears that the chief deficiency that brought about the revolution's defeat lay in that glaring and growing lack brought about by the rapidity of the transition, already discussed, from an Arab agrarian society to a Jewish industrial one. The rapidity of the transformation effectively absented the Arab bourgeoisie and petite bourgeoisie from playing its historic role in the Palestinian national movement at the time, leaving the space open for the feudal-religious patriarchs to take the reins of the movement for a long period, uncontested.

Dr. Abdul-Wahhab al-Kayyali has identified further important causes underpinning the revolution's defeat:

> Weariness from battle, constant military pressure, and hopes that some of the White Paper [of 1939] recommendations would be implemented, as well as the torment of

weapons and ammunition shortages, all of these played a role in hindering the continuation of the revolution. What is more, the world's approach toward the brink of the Second World War drove the French to completely wipe out the revolution's headquarters in Damascus.[105]

To this we can also add two more interconnected factors of key importance in bringing the revolt to an end. The first of these was the role played by Transjordan as then represented by the collaborationist regime of Prince Abdullah; the second was the role played by the agents of counterrevolution inside Palestine, alongside the terrorism of the British and Zionist forces. The way these two factors were interwoven enables us to discuss them simultaneously. The Defense Party led by Ragheb al-Nashashibi was effectively the agent of the collaborationist Transjordanian regime within the Palestinian national movement. Nashahibi's overt connection to Amman camouflaged the Party's more fundamental role as an agent of the British colonizer, an important deception given that this was taking place in the heat of a battle directed primarily at that same British colonizer. As such, the ruse of a primary loyalty to Transjordan was acceptable both to Amman and to London. The Party was basically a small grouping or urban *effendis* primarily representing the interests of the emergent comprador bourgeoisie, which had begun to reveal that the strings behind its presence and growth were in the hands not only of British colonialism, but of the Zionist movement that controlled the Palestinian economy's industrial transformation. This positionality in the class structure is what enables a summation of the Party leadership as follows:

> They collaborated with the [British] occupation on an administrative level, and with the Zionists on a commercial level. They sold land to the Jews and acted as their agents, sowed social divisions and impeded patriotic activity. They made themselves the link between the Hashemites and the

Zionists in 1923–24. They supported the waves of immigration and the Mandate regime throughout the 1920s and supported partition in the 1930s. They called for a Jewish national home to be established on one part of Palestine, and for handing over the remaining part to Transjordan....[106]

In July 1936, the masses east of the Jordan River held a popular conference in the village of Um al-'Amad under the leadership of Mithqal al-Fa'iz in which they decided to give their full support, in terms of material and fighters, to join the Palestine revolution. As Prince Abdullah dedicated his regime's resources to the repression of the movement that developed, the British decided to treat Transjordan as a connected theatre of their war against the Palestinian revolutionaries, especially as it pertained to the movements of revolutionaries. The role played by the collaborationist regime in Amman was not limited to its repression of the Transjordanian mass movement that emerged in support of the revolution. It closed the roads connecting Transjordan to Iraq in order to prevent support arriving from there, and restricted the movements of Palestinian leaders who had been forced to expand their activities in Transjordan after the British sealed off Palestine's northern frontier using barbed wire fencing. Amman crowned its collaborationist and counterrevolutionary resumé when, in 1939, it arrested two Palestinian revolutionary leaders (one of whom was Yusuf Abu Durrah, mentioned above) and handed them over to the British who executed them a few months later. In that period in particular, the Transjordanian regime's forces became especially active alongside British troops and Zionist armed gangs in hunting down revolutionaries.

It is beyond a doubt that this role played by the Transjordanian regime encouraged internal counterrevolutionaries to escalate their own activities. Several leaders of the Defense Party played important roles in setting up what they called the "Peace Teams." These were small bands of mercenaries formed under the auspices of the English, and participated in hunting down and attacking revolutionaries as well as working to dislodge them from fortified positions they held. Fakhri al-Nashashibi was among those who took part in forming, arming, and directing the activities of these teams . . . this is what led to his assassination a few months after the end of the revolution.[107]

Prior to this, the vicious British campaign to disarm the entire Arab population had relied on "encouraging elements hostile to the Mufti to provide [the British] with intelligence, and to identify those involved in the revolution."[108]

The positions of the Iraqi and Saudi regimes at the time were not much better than that of the Transjordanian regime. At the London roundtable conference, both had expressed their readiness "to use the influence they had on Palestinian leaders to put an end to the revolution."[109] None of this, however, was enough to give popular legitimacy and power to Britain's collaborators at the helm of the internal counterrevolution. Quite the opposite, it only served to strengthen the Mufti and his leadership. Moreover, even though a key objective of British support for the counterrevolution was premised on disciplining the Mufti—corralling him into a sheepfold where he could be ultimately controlled—the British never really wavered from the conviction that al-Nashashibi could and would never be a viable alternative to the Mufti. The small margin of maneuver left to the Mufti's leadership, rooted as it was on the partial contradiction between the French colonial regime over Syria/Lebanon and the British Empire, could never hope to bring about a radical change in the balance of power. As soon as this margin of maneuver narrowed on the eve of the Second World War, it became a noose tightening around the Mufti's neck.

Taken together, these realities show that the Palestinian revolution was dealt serious blows at its three vital articulations: its subjective/

internal articulation was devastated by the impotence, inconsistency, weakness, self-centeredness, and ill-coordination of its reactionary leaders; the Arab/regional articulation was incapacitated by the collusion of the Arab regimes with the forces working to undercut the revolution, while the weak Arab popular movements barely engaged with the Palestinian revolution beyond a selective and surface-level participation in the revolution; and the international articulation worked against the revolution at the fundamental level of a balance of power dramatically skewed in favor of the imperial powers, who not only collaborated among themselves, but allied themselves to the Zionist movement, with the result that the Zionists had a considerable striking force at their disposal on the eve of WWII.

The most trustworthy estimate of Arab human casualties over the course of the 1936–1939 Revolution puts the number of those killed and injured over the four-year period at 19,792. The estimate's reliability is partly based on the fact that it is one of the few to include casualties sustained at the hands of the Zionist forces. In its methodology, the estimate relies on the initial, albeit often conservative, accounts cited in official British documents while also cross checking the figures with other sources.[110] According to this study, 1,200 Arabs were killed in 1936; 120 in 1937; 1,200 in 1938; and 1,200 in 1939. The number of Arabs executed over the course of the revolution was 112, and a further 1,200 were killed in various terrorist operations. This adds up to 5,032 Arabs killed over the course of the 1936–1939 Revolution, while the number of those injured in the same period was 14,760 Arabs.* In terms of incarceration, there were around 816 prisoners in 1937; around 2,463 in 1938; and around 5,679 in 1939. The stark significance of these figures can be better appreciated through per capita comparison. If the same human casualties were proportionally inflicted upon British society, it would be the equivalent of

---

*   GK: A study published by *Ma'arakhot* (Vol 55, Issue 55, January–February 1970) states that the 1936–1939 Revolution resulted in a total of 415 Jewish fatalities, out of a total Jewish population of 450,000 people at the time.

200,000 killed, 600,000 injured, and 1,224,000 prisoners. In terms of the United States' population, this would be equivalent to one million killed, three million injured, and over six million incarcerated!

In real terms, and considering the longer-term processes, the more dangerous Arab losses took the form of the rapid growth of the military and economic foundations for the Zionist settler colonial presence in Palestine. It would not be an exaggeration to state that that military and economic presence—that found its densest expression and deepened its ties to imperialism in 1948—established its key bases in the period stretching from 1936 to 1939. One Israeli historian has even gone as far as stating that "the conditions for victory in 1948 were created in the period of the Arab Revolt of 1936."[111]

We can get a sense of the overall policy followed by the Zionists in this period through the fact that they avoided any contradictions arising between them and the British Mandate authorities, even when these authorities—beleaguered as they were by the Arab revolutionaries—had to reject vital demands made by the Zionist movement. The Zionists seem to have held the conviction that did the greatest imaginable service for their own objectives by paving pave the way for the British—and the world's most powerful imperial army at the latter's disposal—to crush the Arab revolution in Palestine. The main Zionist strategies thus followed two parallel paths: first, an alliance with the British to the greatest extent possible (to the point that the Twentieth Zionist Congress held in the summer of 1937 expressed the Zionists' willingness to accept partition to avoid any possible clash with the British, in the hope that the full might of the colonial empire would come crashing down on the Arab revolution that had erupted once again that summer). Second, sustained mobilization of the Zionist communities under Ben-Gurion's "no alternative" slogan, thereby establishing the foundations of a military society and providing it with its martial and economic instruments.

This Zionist insistence on conciliation with the British to the greatest extent possible, despite, for instance, the British imposition of restrictions on Jewish immigration, was a pivotal issue in the history of Zionist politics at the time. Despite the fact that there were several currents within the Zionist movement that completely rejected what was being called "the policy of restraint," the clamorings of these minority currents were unable to change the leadership's strategy. The iron law guiding every step of the Zionist movement at the time was the one summarized by Weizmann when he stated that "there is a complete harmony of interests between Zionism and England in Palestine."

The interplay of the two tenets of Zionist strategy in this period (alliance with the British to the greatest extent possible, and mobilization of the Jewish settler community in Palestine) had devastating consequences. The Jewish bourgeoisie took advantage of the Arab revolution's escalation to put projects in place that would not have been possible under different circumstances. Finding itself suddenly free of the competition from cheap Arab agricultural produce,* this bourgeoisie set out to entrench and develop its economic presence. Naturally, this would have been impossible without the blessing of the British. Over the course of the revolution, the Zionists and the Mandate authorities succeeded in building a network of roads connecting the Jewish settlement colonies to one another and to the major cities. This road network would later form a keystone of Zionist economic infrastructure. Ports played a central role in this infrastructure: the road connecting Haifa and Tel Aviv was paved, the Haifa port was expanded and deepened, and a new port was built in Tel Aviv that would eventually extinguish the vitality of the main Arab port in Yafa. Moreover, the Zionists had a de facto monopoly on the lucrative contracts for provisioning the British troops flooding into Palestine.

Between 1936 and 1939, the Zionists established fifty settlement colonies. In the period between 1936 and 1938, Jewish investment in construction was £1,268,000 for works in five Jewish towns, while

---

* GK: Consider, for instance, the wages in citrus production—the leading agricultural sector in Palestine: the General Agricultural Council declared in 1936 that the annual wage of a Jewish worker per dunam was £12, while the same wage for an Arab worker was £8.

Arab investment in the same period was no more than £120,000 for works in 16 Arab towns. Jewish capital and labor devoted themselves to British security projects aimed at encircling and isolating the Arab revolution. Among these was a barbed wire barrier on the northern and northeastern frontiers of Palestine for which "the British employed Jewish labor at an expenditure of P£100,000 to construct,"[112] as well as dozens of other such projects. Figures appearing in later publications paint an even more accurate picture: the revenues generated by the export of local manufactures nearly doubled between 1935 and 1937 (rising from P£478,807 in 1935 to P£896,875 in 1937) in spite of the disruption caused by the revolution.[113] The only possible explanation for this is the redoubled graft of the Jewish economy.

The scope of this mobilization expanded from the alliance with the Mandate in the economic arena to collusion with the Mandate in the military arena.* The British felt that their Zionist ally was better qualified than any other to play the role of local agent. Ben-Gurion was in fact only telling part of the truth when he admitted that the number of armed Jewish auxiliaries in the police force had risen to 2,863 in September 1936, for that was only a small part of the armed and organized Zionist forces, which also included the Haganah's militants (numbering 12,000 in 1937) and the 3,000 fighters in Ze'ev Jabotinsky's National Military Organization–ETZEL (also known as the Irgun).[114] The alliance of these forces—as the true representatives of the Zionist movement—with British colonialism gave birth to the idea of the Jewish Supernumerary Police (also referred to as the Jewish Auxiliary Police) in the spring of 1936. This provided the pretext for the armed Zionist presence blessed with the full backing and encouragement of British colonial power. After a transition period of a few months, and with full British knowledge and support, the

---

* GK: In his book, *The Making of Israel's Army*, Yigal Allon states: "The years 1937–1939 were the pinnacle of vanguardist settlement and military expansion out into the open... winning important footholds in vitally strategic locations (see Emile Touma's study on this topic published in both *al-Ittihad* and *Fateh* in September 1971).

Haganah initiated a new stage in which it organized its fighting force into patrols and strike forces that carried out targeted attacks against the Arabs with the primary objective of distracting and confusing the revolutionaries. Such an escalation in the role and activity of Zionist military units would not have been possible, while maintaining the "truce" (read: alliance) with the Mandate authorities, had it not been jointly planned and orchestrated between the British and the Zionists. Ben-Gurion himself confirmed that the Jewish Supernumerary Force was an excellent "framework" for the training of the Haganah.[115]

In the summer of 1937, the force was branded the "Jewish Settlement Defense" and later became the "Jewish Settlement Police." It was organized and developed across the country under the tutelage of the British Mandate, who took responsibility for the units' military training. In 1938, the force was augmented by an additional 3,000 recruits. Altogether, these formalized Zionist forces played a direct role in the violent repression of the Arab revolutionaries, especially in the north. In June 1938 the British decided that it behooved them to carry out offensive operations against the revolutionaries, which led them to institute military instruction courses through which large numbers of Haganah units received their training. These units would later form part of the backbone of the Israeli military.[116]

In the early months of 1939, the British army formed ten well-armed Jewish Settlement Police units. Each of the units was given a Hebrew name, and their members were allowed to abandon the official Palestine Police headdress (the *Qalbaq* cap) in favor of the Australian bush hat to further distinguish them. Together, the membership of these units totaled 14,411 men, each led by a British officer whose second-in-command was appointed by the Jewish Agency. In the spring of the same year, 62 mechanized units, each comprised of eight to ten men, were added to the Zionists' military capacity.

In June 1938, the British command had decided to entrust these Jewish forces with the defense of the railways connecting Haifa and al-Lydd that had been the frequent target of Arab guerrilla action. Initially, the British had designated 434 Jewish policemen for the task, but within six months the Jewish Agency succeeded in its efforts to bring this number up to 800. Not only did this development aid in increasing Zionist military capacity, it also helped absorb and employ a large number of unemployed Jewish workers, whose numbers were rapidly increasing in the urban centers. It was in this way that this proletariat was put to work in the apparatus of repression—not just in anti-revolutionary British security projects, but in the emergent Zionist military machine.

In addition to guarding the Haifa–Lydd railway, the British also tasked the Jewish troops with the defense of the Mediterranean pipeline that ran across the Bisan plain and Marj Ibn 'Amer. Construction of the pipeline had just been completed in 1934 with the purpose of carrying crude oil from the Kirkuk oilfields in northern Iraq to Haifa, and had been the target of numerous guerrilla attacks. The particular significance of these attacks was their remarkable symbolic value: the Arab revolutionaries recognized the value of petroleum to the British exploiters, and blew up a section of the pipeline for the first time on July 15, 1937 at a location near Irbid (northern Jordan). They followed this with numerous other attacks, targeting sections of the pipeline near Kawkab al-Hawa, Iksal, 'Afula, Tal al-'Adas, Tamrah, Kufr Misr, Jisr al-Majami', Jinjar, Bisan, and Indur ('Ain Dawr). The British proved unable to defend this vitally strategic pipeline, explicitly stating this inability on several occasions, while the *"masoorah,"* as the Arab peasants called it, became enshrined in folklore glorifying acts of popular heroism.

At any rate, the British did finally ensure a minimum level of protection for the pipeline in two ways: they tasked the Jewish gangs with guarding the pipeline within the Mandate borders of Palestine, while in Transjordan they entrusted this task to "Shaikh Turki ibn Zain, patriarch of the al-Zain branch of the Bani Sakhr tribe, who was authorized to patrol the desert by any means necessary by the [Iraqi Petroleum] Company."[117]

These specific developments were of the utmost importance, as they reinforced the British conviction that the formation of an effective Zionist offensive force would solve many of the problems relating to securing imperial interests more broadly. Ben-Gurion practically spells this out with unmitigated candor in his recollection of the efforts expended by the British to establish an armed Jewish force specifically tasked with the protection of these interests. In this vein, it was the British officer Charles Orde Wingate who played a particularly prominent role in translating the British–Zionist alliance into a pragmatic reality. Though Zionist historians have tried to intimate that Wingate's efforts were the result of an idiosyncratic temperament combined with an "idealistic" devotion to the Zionist cause, it is actually quite clear that this British military intelligence officer was sent by his chiefs to Haifa in the autumn of 1937 with a very specific mission. The armed Jewish strike force had been established at least six months prior, but still needed preparation and development. Wingate's task was to set this enhancement of Zionist military capacity in motion.

Widely considered by Israeli military figures as the true founder of the Israeli army, Captain Wingate made it his primary mission to safeguard the oil pipeline. But this mission soon expanded to a series of murderous terrorist raids on Arab communities that this British officer zealously took it upon himself to teach his pupils at Indur—Moshe Dayan among them—to perfect. There is no doubt that in addition to his competence as a seasoned imperial officer, Wingate was armed with boundless racist hatred of Arabs. His biography, as related by those who worked with him, suggests that he took great pleasure in killing, torturing, and degrading Arab peasants.[118] In his study of Yigal Allon's history of the Israeli military, Emile Touma confirms that Wingate and his coterie of brutes systematically worked to aid British forces by terrorizing the Arab inhabitants of the rural areas during the 1936–1939 Revolution.

Through imperialist men-on-the-spot like Wingate, and reactionary leaders like Prince Abdullah and the members of his ruling class, the British were able to pave the way militarily and economically for the Zionist movement to assume a position as the advance-guard protecting British imperial interests. This process developed alongside the British camp's certainty that the Palestinian national movement was not in a state of revolutionary-ness that would enable it to take on this united front of enemies. The British were thus able to arrive in this early moment at the strategy that the US would, thirty years later, call "Vietnamization." In the midst of all of this, the Palestinian national movement—incapacitated as it was by the internal factors discussed above, as well as the violent assaults of the British and the Zionists—found itself in critical condition on the eve of the Second World War.

The claim by some historians that the Arabs "put a halt" to their revolution to allow Britain, once again, the chance to wage its world war against Nazism is, at best, naïve. Not only is such a claim invalidated by the record of events, but also by the fact that Hajj Amin al-Husseini himself sought refuge in Nazi Germany throughout the years of the war.

We need to take all of the foregoing processes as a totality to understand the realities of the political and social map of the situation that prevailed in the years between 1936 and 1939. Only by appreciating all of these processes, and the dialectical relations that connected them, can we explain the state of stagnation that marked the Palestinian national movement throughout the years of the war. As the Second World War came to an end, the British saw that the movement had been all but completely domesticated: those who were at its head had been smashed and scattered; its base had been exhausted, the social fabric of the Arab community frayed—worn thin by the violent social transformation underway—and as a result of the organizational and mobilizational failures of its leaders and political parties, and also due to the weakness and stupefaction of the Left, and the insipidness of the nationalist movement in the Arab countries.

And so it was that the Zionist movement in Palestine entered the 1940s with barely an obstacle on the battlefield. By the end of the world war, the international climate was particularly favorable to Zionist ambitions given the atmosphere of psychological and political sympathy that proliferated as Hitler's criminal massacres of Jews came to light. The Arab regimes that surrounded it were bourgeois regimes embroiled in a historical crisis, and lacked any real power. Nor was there in Palestine's Jewish community at the time an effective leftist movement that could push against the force of the Zionist current; it was, for the most part, a society imbued with the ethos of the settler colonist. For its part, the Palestinian Left had, since the Second World War, lost the spark that had ignited some of its dynamism in the mid-1930s. This loss was due to the change of the Comintern's Palestine policy combined with the failure to Arabize the Palestine Communist Party. Furthermore, the communist Left had been increasingly subjected to the repression of the defeated Arab leadership. The Mufti's henchmen, for instance, assassinated the labor organizer Sami Taha in Haifa on September 12, 1947, just as they had assassinated Michel Mitri, one of the main organizers of the 1936 workers' strikes, on December 22, 1936.

All these factors combined in the mid-1940s to prepare the ground for the Zionist movement to dramatically escalate what had, up until then, been a partial contradiction with British colonialism in Palestine after many eventful years of alliance. By 1947, conditions were ripe for the Zionists to harvest the fruit of the 1936 Revolution's defeat, a harvest delayed by the Second World War. As such, the second chapter of the revolution's defeat—from late 1947 to mid-1948—was remarkable for its brevity: it was only the epilogue to a long and bloody chapter endured from April 1936 to September 1939.

AFTERWORD

GHASSAN KANAFANI: PIONEER IN THE STUDY OF THE GREAT PALESTINIAN REVOLUTION OF 1936-1939

In the early 1930s, Palestine witnessed a series of transformations that, on the one hand, aimed to consolidate the Jewish national home project, and on the other hand, created the conditions for the outbreak of the Great Palestinian Revolution. After Hitler came to power in Germany in 1933, the growing waves of hostility and persecution of the Jewish population led to a boom in the Jewish immigration movement to Palestine. In 1935 alone, about sixty-two thousand Jewish immigrants arrived in Palestine, among whom were a number of established Jewish capitalists, skilled workers, and technicians. This gave the European Jewish economy a strong boost at the expense of the Arab economy, which was already suffering from a suffocating crisis. The tendency of European Jewish institutions to appropriate large areas of Arab land led to the emergence of a new social group in the Palestinian countryside, the category of landless peasants, and to an increase in the phenomenon of migration from the countryside to the city in search of paid work. All this at a time when Palestinian cities were suffering due to the exacerbation of unemployment in the ranks of the Arab workers, a result of the expansion of the Hebrew labor policy implemented by Zionist organizations.

In the atmosphere of this intense competition, many indicators foretold the growth of revolutionary feelings among the Palestinian Arab people, as well as their increased hostility to British colonialism.

The struggle of Arab workers escalated, the size of their trade union organizations expanded, and labor garrisons were formed to confront the Histadrut policy aimed at expelling Arab workers from their workplaces. Many bloody battles broke out between destitute peasants, policemen, and Jewish settlers. Forms of organization of the Arab national movement advanced with the emergence of political blocs, led by young revolutionary elements in the major cities, and some armed Ansar squads began to spread in the mountains, the most prominent of which was the squad formed by Sheikh Izz al-Din al-Qassam, whose death in November 1935 during a confrontation with the British forces had a deep impact on all of Palestine that contributed to urging revolution—especially since many of his supporters were still ready to take up arms to resist the Zionist project of a Jewish national home and British colonialism at the first opportunity they had.

The general strike broke out spontaneously in Palestine in 1936 as a result of the accumulated feelings of anger and frustration among the Palestinian Arabs over many years. It also came in the midst of an anti-colonial revolutionary wave that swept a number of Arab countries, especially Egypt and Syria, between 1935 and 1936.

Fearing that the leadership of the strike would be transferred to the hands of the local field leaders who had joined the framework of national committees in the main cities, the leaders of the Arab parties met on April 25, 1936 and announced the formation of the "Arab Higher Committee" headed by the Mufti of Jerusalem, Mohammed Amin al-Husseini. It called for the continuation of the general strike until the British government fundamentally changed its policy and responded to three Arab demands: a complete halt to Jewish immigration; the prevention of the land transfers to the Jews; and the formation of a national government responsible to a representative council. On May 15, in the face of the continued intransigence of the British authorities, Palestinians took up acts of civil disobedience and refrained from paying taxes, and armed groups of supporters began to appear in the mountains and countryside, attacking the British military forces and Zionist colonies.

On October 12, 1936, six months after the outbreak of the general strike, the Arab Higher Committee succeeded in persuading the representatives of the popular groups in the national committees to stop the strike and the revolutionary movement, responding to a number of Arab kings and princes who called on Palestinians to "rely on the good will of our friend Great Britain, who promised she would do justice." However, the British government's refusal to respond to the Arab demands reignited the armed revolution in late September 1937. This made the British authorities consider the Arab Higher Committee as an illegal organization, and so they excluded the Mufti of Jerusalem from the presidency of the Supreme Islamic Sharia Council, arrested a number of leaders, and exiled them to the Seychelles, though Mohammed Amin al-Husseini succeeded in escaping by sea to Lebanon.

In order to halt the revolution, the British Mandate authorities resorted to the harshest methods of repression and put an emergency law into effect, imposing martial law, summoning new military units from Malta, and exploiting family disputes, especially between the Husseini and Nashashibi families, to stir up a state of internal strife among the Palestinians. It also decided to legitimize the Zionist paramilitary organization Haganah by recruiting guards to protect the Jewish settler colonies, and started maneuvering politically, forming a royal commission to investigate the events headed by Lord Peel and going to Palestine to issue a report on July 7, 1937 that did not meet any of the Arab demands. Rather than the three original proposals, it suggested dividing Palestine into two states: an Arab one to be annexed to the Emirate of Transjordan, and a Jewish one whose doors would be open to Jewish immigration. The religious and strategic parts of Palestine would remain under British control, provided that the Mandate system be replaced by a system of treaties with the Arab and Jewish states.

The overwhelming majority of Palestinian Arabs strongly rejected the report, forcing the British government to admit its inability to implement its own proposals, and prompting it, in November 1938, to invite representatives of the Arabs of Palestine, of the neighboring Arab countries, and of the Jewish Agency to deliberate with them on the next policy. On this basis, the London conference was inaugurated on February 7, 1939 in the presence of representatives of Arabs and Jews. This conference failed to reconcile the two parties, so the British government issued, on May 17, 1939, the "white paper" that proposed the creation of an independent Palestinian government over ten years, in which Arabs and Jews could participate, linked with Britain by a treaty that guaranteed the commercial and military interests of the two countries. There would also be consultations with the League of Nations with a view to end the Mandate, provided that 75,000 Jewish immigrants would be allowed to enter over the next five years and the British High Commissioner would be granted the authority to prevent and regulate the transfer of land. The Zionist leaders completely rejected this white paper, as did the head of the "Arab Higher Committee" Hajj Mohammed Amin al-Husseini.

With the issuance of the White Paper, the revolution had begun to suffer from severe weaknesses as a result of the inability of the revolutionaries to obtain weapons and ammunition, the exacerbation of internal strife among the Palestinians, and the martyrdom, withdrawal, and arrest of a number of prominent revolutionaries. In fact, the years 1936–39 were the period in which the fate of Palestine was decided. During that period, the political, economic, and military power of the Jewish settler community was strengthened on the one hand, and, on the other hand, the Palestinian national movement was hit hard, as its military strength was destroyed, and its leadership was dispersed from the landowners and from the merchants of the towns.

✻✻✻✻✻

While the study of the Great Palestinian Revolution has attracted the attention of Palestinian and foreign historians in recent years, Ghassan Kanafani had tackled the study of that revolution and the analysis of the reasons for its defeat since the early seventies of the twentieth century.

In this lengthy study, "The 1936–1939 Revolution in Palestine: Backgrounds, Details and Analysis" (*Palestinian Affairs*, Issue 6, January 1972, pp. 45–77), Ghassan Kanafani estimated that one of the main reasons for the defeat of that revolution was the nature of its leaders, which he described as "semi-feudal–semi-religious." He argued that their success in imposing their hegemony over the Palestinian national movement before the Nakba was due to two interrelated reasons. The first being two-fold, in that "the presence and effectiveness of the Zionist movement, elevated the national cause above all other causes and struggles in Palestinian society. Indeed, the challenge posed by the Zionist movement imposed itself upon the Arab working classes, which had suffered directly and daily as a consequence of the British Empire-backed Zionist invasion."[119] The second reason being that there was "an abnormal limit on the contradiction between British imperialism and the local Arab leadership composed of feudal-religious family patriarchs. Such a leadership would usually, under circumstances that differed from the particularity of the Palestinian case, find its class interests best served by a near-total alliance with imperialism."[120] As a result of these two reasons, the struggle of the Palestinian people enjoyed a distinction that "made it, at that time, differ from the struggles of the Arab peoples across the region." Ghassan Kanafani noted that the "feudal-clerical" leaders who rose to the top of the movement of the Arab masses and thwarted the Palestinian national struggle, also benefited from the "insipidness of the fledgling urban Arab bourgeoisie and the limited contradiction that had developed between these patriarchs and British imperialism, which focused its energies on its alliance"[121] with the Zionist movement and its religious characteristics, as well as from the small size of the Arab proletariat and the atrophy of its Communist Party.

On the other hand, if the Arab peasant benefitted—as Kanafani argued—the debts that the *"effendiyya"* offered him, then for the peasant this constituted "an evil less deadly than the evil of Zionism."[122] Ottoman rule did not amount to uprooting them and the institutions that have grown since ancient times around these relations (family, clan, sect, etc.) from their land. In such conditions, "it was impossible for the liberation movement to neglect the primary national dimension of the struggle," just as, "in confronting the tremendous religious fervor evident in every manifestation of the Zionist colonialization of Palestine, the backwards countryside could not but barricade itself behind politicized religiosity as a central facet of its battle against Zionist-imperial conquest."[123]

Ghassan Kanafani paid great attention to the great Revolution of 1936–1939 and presented this pioneering and comprehensive study because he recognized that it was the defeat of that revolution that paved the way for the occurrence of the Palestinian Nakba in 1948.

—Maher al-Charif
2022

GLOSSARY

1967 War

The 1967 War was a conflict that took place between June 5 and June 10, 1967, after Israel launched a preemptive strike on the Egyptian Air Force. This surprise attack was followed by ground offensives against Egypt, Jordan, and Syria, resulting in the displacement of over three hundred thousand Palestinians from their homes and significant territorial gains for Israel, including the occupation of the Sinai Peninsula and the Golan Heights, and solidifying the occupation of the West Bank and Gaza. This defeat played a significant role in the fragmentation of the Arab National Movement and made more space for the Zionist settler movement, but also urged the revolutionary and armed currents of the Palestinian resistance.

Aqsa Mosque

Al-Aqsa Mosque, which includes the Dome of the Rock as well as the silver-domed al-Qibli prayer hall, is an Islamic site in occupied East Jerusalem where unsolicited visits, prayers and rituals by non-Muslims are forbidden according to decades-long international agreements. In the past few years, there have been regular instances of raids and invasions of the mosque compound by Jewish far-right groups consisting of hundreds of extremist settlers and fanatical Zionists and accompanied by Israeli security forces. In June 2023, legislators of the ruling Likud party proposed to divide Al-Aqsa to be allotted to settlers and Palestinians separately.

Arab Higher Committee (AHC)

The AHC was formed in 1936 by Hajj Mohammed Amin al-Husseini to coordinate and lead political, economic, and social affairs of the Arab population under British Mandatory rule. Its members included many from the intellectual and political class, and played a significant albeit often contradictory role in the coordination of the 1936 general strike. It also opened offices in several Arab capitals to solicit support and buy arms. Although it was disbanded by the British in 1937 and many of its leaders were exiled or arrested, an AHC office in Beirut continued to operate until al-Husseini's death in 1974.

Arab Nationalist Movement (ANM)

The Arab Nationalist Movement (ANM) was born out of the growing student movement in Lebanon during the early 1950s, cofounded by George Habash, whose family had to flee to Lebanon after the Nakba. Habash articulated the idea that Arab unity was key for defeating Zionism in the region and achieving the full liberation of Palestine from Israeli settlers. The Popular Front for the Liberation of Palestine (PFLP) was born out of this organization.

Balfour Declaration

The Balfour Declaration was a public statement issued on November 2, 1917 by the British government during World War I. It contained a letter from Arthur Balfour, the British Foreign Secretary, to Lord Lionel Walter Rothschild, conveying the British government's commitment to facilitating the creation of a Jewish homeland in Palestine. It is considered to be a pivotal movement of British support for the Zionist movement, while the Palestinian Arab population considered it to be a betrayal of their right to self-determination.

British Emergency Regulations

The British Emergency Regulations were a set of policies established in 1945 and enforced during the British Mandate period intended to repress and control the movement against British and Zionist occupation. They included powers such as the ability to arrest and detain without trial or charge, censorship of publications, control over any form of organization, and curfews and restriction of movement; all tactics that are quite similar to those used by the Zionist forces against the Palestinian population today.

British Mandate

The British Mandate refers to the period of 1920 to 1948 of British military occupation and administration of the Palestinian territory, established following the defeat of the Ottoman Empire in World War I. Under the terms of the Mandate, Britain exercised political, administrative, and military control over Palestine and its peoples, and employed this control to facilitate European Jewish immigration and the establishment of a Jewish national home in Palestine. The Mandate ended in 1948 following the United Nation's approval of a partition plan that established a separate Jewish state on 56 percent of Palestinian territory.

Cairo Agreement

The Cairo Agreement, or the Cairo Accord, was an agreement made in 1969 between Emile Bustani, Commander of the Lebanese Armed Forces, and Yasser Arafat, Chairman of the Palestine Liberation Organization, and was brokered by Gamal Abdel Nasser, President of Egypt. The text of the agreement, which was intended to remain secret but was leaked in 1970 by the Lebanese newspaper *Annahar*, set terms for the official approval for Palestinian forces to waged their armed revolutionary struggle from within Lebanon, where a large number of Palestinians had already been living due to displacement. It was repealed by the Lebanese government in 1987.

Charles Orde Wingate

Charles Orde Wingate (1903–1944) was a British military officer who led and trained special forces units in Palestine, known as Special Night Squads or the Special Interrogation Group, working very closely with local Jewish forces, that used guerrilla warfare tactics and intelligence gathering to disrupt Arab revolutionary activities. An admirer of the Zionist movement, Wingate strongly advocated for Jewish settlement and for the formation of Jewish military units.

David Ben-Gurion

David Ben-Gurion (1886–1973) is considered the national founder of the illegal state of Israel and served as the first Prime Minister from 1955 to 1963. Ben-Gurion came from a family of Zionists and was a leader in the consolidation of pro-Israeli forces and in the establishment of the Israeli state. He believed strongly in the expansion of a Zionist state and strategized for the expansion of the Israeli state even beyond the occupied territory of Palestine.

effendi/effendiyya

An Ottoman term used to address or refer to an individual of the intellectual or professional class, or with a government appointment.

Emile Bustani

Emile Bustani (1909–2002) served as the Commander of the Lebanese Armed Forces from 1965 to 1970. In 1969, in a deal brokered by Egyptian President Gamal Abdel Nasser, Bustani and Yasser Arafat, then-chairman of the Palestine Liberation Organization, reached an agreement known as the Cairo Agreement, which was drafted by Bustani.

foco

Foco or *foco guerrillero* is a concept that refers to the style of rural guerrilla warfare that is organized through units of small, well-organized fighters that launch armed struggle against repressive forces, that serves as a revolutionary nucleus to mobilize and give optimism to the masses in struggle. This theory, popularized by Che Guevara, was employed in different ways in various national liberation struggles across the world.

Gamal Abdel Nasser

Gamal Abdel Nasser (1918–1970) was born in Alexandria, Egypt, under the rule of the British-backed Egyptian monarchy. In 1952, Nasser, along with other members of the Egyptian army, together known as the Free Officers, led the Egyptian Revolution of 1952 that ousted King Farouk. Nasser became President of Egypt in 1956, a position he served until his death. By the end of 1957, Nasser had nationalized all previous British and French assets in Egypt. He is remembered as a prominent leader in attempting to unite the region, in both Pan Arab and Pan African processes, and along with Kwame Nkruma (Ghana), Josip Broz Tito (Yugoslavia), Sukarno (Indonesia) and Jawaharlal Nehru (India), played a leading role in the early days of the Non-Aligned Movement.

George Habash

George Habash (1926–2008) was a Palestinian political leader who founded the Popular Front for the Liberation of Palestine (PFLP) and served as its General Secretary from 1967 to 2000. When asked to define the strategy of the Arab Nationalist Movement (ANM), Habash cited Che Guevara's speech on the formation of a new human necessary for the resistance and defense of a socialist society.

Haganah

The Haganah was a Jewish paramilitary organization that operated under the British Mandate until the establishment of the state of Israel. It began operating clandestinely under the British, organizing and facilitating illegal Jewish immigration to Palestine and launching attacks against Arab organizations, but soon began to cooperate more openly with British forces, particularly during World War II. It was responsible for many massacres of Palestinian communities and the destruction of villages, especially during the 1948 Nakba. It served as the foundation for the Israeli Defense Forces (IDF), which continues to use similar tactics against the Palestinian population today.

Hajj Mohammed Amin al-Husseini

Hajj Mohammed Amin al-Husseini (1895–1974) was an Islamic cleric who rose to the position of Grand Mufti of Jerusalem in 1921 with British approval. Soon disillusioned by the false promises of the British, he emerged as a major but disputed leader of the Palestinian national movement and went into exile in 1937 after escaping arrest. In 1941, he was granted asylum in Italy and there made official requests for support from both Hitler and Mussolini for support against Zionist settlement, and directly collaborated with the Nazis in WWII. After the 1948 Nakba, he attempted to lead a new Palestinian government first in Gaza and then Cairo. He was expelled from Egypt in 1954, and died in Lebanon in 1974.

Histadrut

Founded in 1920, the Histadrut promoted a current of Zionism known as Labor Zionism, which pushed for Jewish workers to settle in Palestine and to displace the local Arab economy, the working class in particular, in order to form the basis for Zionism's Jewish national project. It played a major role in shifting the opinion of the early Jewish immigrants—many of whom were influenced by Orthodox Jewish, Marxist, and Socialist anti-Zionism—away from progressive ideas, and towards the nationalism that of the Zionist project by funneling members of the Jewish working class in Palestine into military and state institutions. By 1939, its membership reached approximately one hundred thousand, or 75 percent of all Jewish workers in Mandatory Palestine. It remains one of the most influential Israeli national institutions today, and a cornerstone of Israel's regime of institutionalized racism against the indigenous Palestinian population.

Izz al-Din al-Qassam

Izz al-Din al-Qassam (1882–1935) was born in Syria, spent his early years studying to become an imam, and became involved in anti-colonial activities against the Italian invasion of Libya and the French occupation of Syria. He arrived in Haifa in the early 1920s and joined the struggle against the British occupation of Palestine, organizing and leading early forms of armed struggle that conducted attacks on British and Zionist military and police stations, as well as settlements. He was martyred in 1935 after a ten-day manhunt by the British police. His funeral, which became a mass demonstration of Arab unity against colonialism, was attended by over three thousand Palestinians, the majority from the peasant and working classes. Strikes were held in various Palestinian and Syrian cities in reaction to his assassination. His defiance inspired revolutionary sentiment and armed struggle in the Palestinian and Arab populations until today.

Jewish Supernumerary Police/Jewish Auxiliary Police

The Jewish Supernumerary Police was a police force that operated during the British Mandatory period, comprised of Jewish individuals who volunteered or were recruited to assist British authorities in repressing Arab anti-colonial activities.

kuffiya

An Arab headdress made of a square piece of fabric, with a pattern of checks or stripes, most commonly black and white or red and white. Traditionally it was worn to protect the head and face from the elements, but it has become a symbol associated with Palestinian nationalism and solidarity, and is often worn as a political statement.

Moshe Dayan

Moshe Dayan (1915–1981) began his military career in the Haganah during the 1936–1939 Revolution. He quickly rose through the ranks and became a military leader in 1948. Following the establishment of the state of Israel, he served as the Israeli Defense Forces' (IDF) chief of staff from 1953 to 1958, and was acting minister of defense during the 1967 War, orchestrating the occupation of the remaining Palestinian territories as well as the Sinai Peninsula and the Golan Heights.

Mufti

An Islamic religious scholar that is authorized to issue legal opinions on issues of religious affairs.

Nahda

Also known as the Arab Awakening, the Nahda refers to a cultural and intellectual movement in the late nineteenth and early twentieth century that emerged as a response to the cultural and ideological challenges of European colonialism after the fall of the Ottoman Empire. The Nahda was characterized by a revitalization of Arab cultural and intellectual life, with many writers, poets, and scholars reviving Arab language, literature, and education.

Nakba

The beginning of the Nakba ("The Catastrophe") is remembered every May 15th, the day in 1948 when the illegal state of Israel was declared. To make way for the Israeli state, over eight hundred thousand Palestinians were forcibly displaced and their homes, farms, and lands were stolen. However, the process of the Nakba is considered ongoing as the policy of assassination, detainment, displacement, terror, land theft, and denial of refugee return perpetrated by Zionist forces and supported by the United States continues.

National Military Organization—ETZEL

ETZEL was a Jewish paramilitary faction within the Haganah that represented an even more right-wing Zionist current that advocated against any compromises or negotiation with British or Arab parties.

It conducted many high-profile attacks on both British targets and Arab communities. After 1948, it was integrated into the Israeli Defense Forces, and many former members went on to hold prominent positions in the Israeli military and government. Its last commander, Menachem Begin (1913–1992), was Israel's prime minister from 1977–1983.

Palestine Communist Party (PCP)

Established in 1923, the Palestinian Communist Party was initially composed of mainly leftist Jewish members, but in the 1930s, began to attract an Arab membership. Initially it proposed class solidarity between Arab and Jewish workers against the British Mandate, but as Zionism grew in strength, it shifted towards supporting Arab nationalism and opposing Zionist settlement. The PCP allied itself with the Soviet Union and joined the Comintern in the early 1930s until the Comintern's dissolution in 1943.

Palestinian Arab Workers' Society (PAWS)

Founded in 1925, the Palestinian Arab Workers' Society was the main Arab labor organization during the time of the British mandate and organized the first national labor congress in 1930. Sami Taha served as general secretary from 1937 until he was assassinated in 1947. PAWS played a significant role in mobilizing Arab workers across various sectors, particularly during the 1936 general strike, and initiated collective actions to push for fair working conditions, against the wage discrimination faced by the Arab population, and for social welfare.

Palestine Liberation Organization (PLO)

The Palestine Liberation Organization—formed in 1964 with the stated purpose of liberating Palestine—is an umbrella organization with representatives from multiple political parties, resistance groups and mass organizations. Today, Palestinian Authority President Mahmoud

Abbas' party, Fatah, is the largest organization in the PLO. The Popular Front for the Liberation of Palestine is the largest left-wing grouping.

Peel Commission

A few weeks after the outbreak of a general strike on April 19, 1936, the British government set up an official commission of inquiry under Lord Peel. It arrived in Jerusalem on November 11, 1936, and began its inquiries, which resulted in a report published by the government on July 7, 1937. The report included a recommendation that Palestine be partitioned into two states, an Arab state to be annexed to Transjordan, and an Israeli state. The British maintained their mandate over strategic religious sites in Palestine.

Popular Front for the Liberation of Palestine (PFLP)

The PFLP was founded in 1967 by George Habash as a revolutionary Marxist–Leninist organization. The program of the PFLP calls for the establishment of a democratic, secular, and socialist state in all of Palestine, defends the right to armed struggle and resistance, and does not recognize the legitimacy of an Israeli state.

United Nations Relief and Works Agency (UNRWA)

The United Nations Relief and Works Agency for Palestine Refugees in the Near East (UNRWA) is a UN agency that was established to support the relief and human development of Palestinian refugees. The UNRWA was established in 1949 after the Nakba and is a subsidiary organ of the UN General Assembly. For decades, Israel and its supporters in the United States have attacked the UNRWA and its funding has been cut to the point where its ability to provide basic services to refugees is at severe risk.

Wadi' al-Bustani

Wadi' al-Bustani (1888–1945) was a prominent intellectual born in Lebanon who played a pivotal role in the Nahda. He worked briefly for the British Mandate government during World War I, but soon resigned and joined the Palestinian nationalist movement, for some years working as a lawyer to defend the land rights of Palestinian farmers. He is well known for his poetry and translations of many classics of literature from India into Arabic.

White Paper of 1939

Officially titled "Statement of Policy Regarding Palestine," the White Paper was a British policy document issued in 1939 that attempted to respond to escalating tensions between Jewish immigrants and Palestinian Arabs by proposing restrictions on Jewish immigration, land transfers, and the establishment of an independent Palestinian state. It was rejected by the Zionist movement for not guaranteeing a Jewish state, and the Palestinian national movement for not addressing their demands for self-determination.

Yasser Arafat

Yasser Arafat (1929–2004) was a Palestinian political leader who cofounded the armed resistance group Fatah and served as Chairman of the Palestinian Liberation Organization (PLO) from 1969 until his death. Though he is remembered by many across the world as a leader of the Palestinian cause, he is also highly criticized for the controversial signing of the Oslo Accords: the culmination of the US-sponsored "peace process" from 1993–2000 that formalized the Israeli state within 1967 borders, officially dividing Palestine into disconnected territories and ushering in an era of neoliberalism with dire consequences for the Palestinian liberation movement today.

Yehuda Bauer

Yehuda Bauer (1926–) was born in Czechoslovakia and is a Zionist historian of the Holocaust. In 1939 his family immigrated to Palestine and he fought as a member of the Zionist forces during the Nakba. Bauer was one of the main architects of the International Holocaust

Remembrance Alliance (IHRA) definition of antisemitism, which classifies Palestinian political positions on sovereignty and the right to return as antisemitic.

zajal

A traditional form of Arabic poetry that originated in the Levant region, typically improvised.

Zionism

Zionism refers to a political and ideological movement that emerged in the late nineteenth century with the aim of establishing a Jewish homeland in the historical region of Palestine, and today supports the continued existence and expansion of Israel as this state. The first Zionist Congress was held in Basel, Switzerland in 1897 and resulted in the formation of the World Zionist Organization under the leadership of Theodor Herzl.

Zionist Congress (1937)

The Twentieth Zionist Congress was held in Basel, Switzerland in 1937 to discuss and respond to the Peel Commission report. It revealed many divisions within the Zionist movement, as some rejected the Peel Commission's partition plan, while others supported continued cooperation with Britain. Ultimately, a special committee known as the Sachar Committee was established to study the proposal and its implications.

CONTRIBUTORS

GHASSAN KANAFANI was a political activist, artist, and writer who gave his life for the Palestinian people. He took part in founding the Popular Front for the Liberation of Palestine (PFLP), and is the accomplished author of many short stories, novels, plays, articles, and studies. Kanafani was assassinated in Beirut by the Israeli Mossad in 1972.

HAZEM JAMJOUM is a translator and audio archivist living in London, United Kingdom.

LAYAN SIMA FULEIHAN is a popular educator and organizer. She is the Education Director of The People's Forum and an editor at 1804 Books in New York City.

MAHER AL-CHARIF is Head of the Research Department at the Institute for Palestine Studies, Associate Researcher at the French Institute for the Near East, and Lecturer at the Faculty of Letters and Human Sciences at Saint Joseph University.

ACKNOWLEDGMENTS

This book would not have been possible without the support and contributions of many comrades across the world. In particular, many thanks to the editors of 1804 Books for their careful review and suggestions. To Vijay Prashad, Sudhanva Deshpande, and Ghassane Koumiya for their guidance and political insight. To Hazem Jamjoum for a beautiful translation that brings Ghassan Kanafani's voice together with his analysis to the English language. To Hannah Priscilla-Craig and Vivek Venkatraman for the thoughtful interior and exterior designs that evoke the importance and urgency of reading this text today. To Anni Kanafani and her children, for their love and care for Ghassan Kanafani's legacy and their commitment to making his contributions available to all who share his struggle. And to all the comrades of the International Peoples' Assembly for their support and solidarity, especially their dedication to the Palestinian cause of liberation.

The translator would like to thank Ameera Kawash, Mohammed el-Kurd, Frida Wahbeh, Mohammad Jamjoum, and Mohamed Masoud for their support and insights with the translation.

ENDNOTES

Originally published in "شؤون فلسطينية" (Palestinian Affairs) *Issue #6 (January 1972).*

An earlier English translation of this essay was prepared by the Central Media Unit of the Popular Front for the Liberation of Palestine in 1974, and is published on https://www.marxists.org/archive/kanafani/1972/revolt.htm

This translation is prepared from the text's publication in Arabic in the volume الدراسات السياسية المجلّد الخامس *(Ghassan Kanafani's Political Studies) by Rimal Books, with permission from Ghassan Kanafani's heirs.*

The Palestinian Cause is a Banner for All of Humanity

1. "Cairo Agreement between the Lebanese Authorities and the Palestinian Guerrilla Organizations," Interactive Encyclopedia of the Palestine Question, November 3, 1969, https://www.palquest.org/en/historictext/9625/cairo-agreement-between-lebanese-authorities-and-palestinian-guerrilla-organizations.
2. Abdul-Wahhab Kayyali, *Palestine: A Modern History,* First edition (London: Third World Centre for Research and Pub., 1981), 231.
3. Louis Brehony, "Ghassan Kanafani: Voice of Palestine (1936-1972)," *Palestine Chronicle* (blog), September 4, 2017, https://www.palestinechronicle.com/ghassan-kanafani-voice-of-palestine-1936-1972/.
4. Kanafani, "Ghassan Kanafani Interviewed in 1972."
5. Ghassan Kanafani, *On Zionist Literature* (Ebb Books, 2022).
6. Nadezhda Krupskaya, *How Lenin Studied Marx* (Labour Monthly Pamphlet No. 2, 1933), https://www.marxists.org/archive/krupskaya/works/howleninstudiedmarx.htm.
7. Ghassan Kanafi, *The Revolution of 1936-1939 in Palestine,* (1804 Books, 2023), p.27
8. Anni Kanafani, أني كنفاني: أتخيل غسان يجلس معنا ["I Imagine Ghassan Sitting with Us"], July 20, 2022, https://www.palestine-studies.org/ar/node/1652961.
9. Brehony, "Kanafani: Voice of Palestine."

THE REVOLUTION OF 1936-1939 IN PALESTINE

Background: The Workers

10 Said Himadeh (ed.) *Economic Organization of Palestine*. American University of Beirut. Beirut 1939, p.32.
11 Moshe Menuhin, *The Decadence of Judaism in Our Time* (Beirut: Institute of Palestine Studies), 1969.
12 Nathan Weinstock, *Le Sionisme - Contra Israel* (Paris: Maspero, 1969).
13 Ibid.
14 Himadeh, p.26, 27.
15 Weinstock, Op. cit.
16 Himadeh, Op. cit., p.373.
17 Ibid. p.376.
18 *Collection of Arab Testimonies in Palestine before the British Royal Commission*. Al-Itidal Press Damascus, 1938, p.54.
19 Ibid. p.55.
20 Himadeh. Op. cit. (the number of the unemployed increased to 4,000 in Yafa alone after 1936. See footnote 5, p.55).
21 *Collection*. Op. cit, p.55.
22 Ibid. p.55. An article in issue #3460 of the Israeli newspaper *Davar* puts Histadrut membership at 150,000 workers at the end of September 1936. The government report on the year 1935 puts Histadrut membership at 74,000 at the end of 1935.
23 *Davar* No. 3462 (See ft. note 13. p.661.)
24 *Collection*. p.15.
25 Ibid., p.66.
26 Ibid., p.59.
27 Yehuda Bauer, "The Arab Revolt of 1936" *New Outlook*. Vol. 9 No. 6 (81). Tel-Aviv, 1966. p. 50.
28 Ibid., p.51.
29 In 1930, the number of Arab construction workers in Jerusalem dropped from 1,500 to 500 while that of Jews went up from 550 to 1,600.
30 Up to 1931, the Zionists expelled 20,000 Palestinian Arab peasants after they bought the land on which the latter used to work.
31 Haim Hanagbi, Moshe Machover, Akiva Orr, "The Class Nature of Israel" *New Left Review* (65), Jan–Feb 1971, p.6.
32 Theodor Herzl, *Selected Works Vol 7, Book 1* (Tel Aviv: Newman Ed), p.86.
33 Exco Foundation for Palestine, Inc., Palestine. *A Study of Jewish, Arab and British Policies. Vol. 1.* Yale University Press. 1947. p. 561.
34 Abdul-Wahhab Kayyali, *Modern History of Palestine*, (Beirut: Arab Institute of Studies and Publication, 1970), p. 174.
35 *Documents of the Palestine Arab Resistance* (1918–1939). Beirut, pp. 22. 23. 24, 25.
36 "Action among the peasants and the struggle against Zionism, The Palestine Communist Party Theses for 1931." *Communist Internationalism and the Arab Revolution*, Dar al-Haqiqa, Beirut, p. 54.
37 Ibid., pp. 122, 121.
38 Ibid., pp. 124.

Background: The Peasants

39 Ibid., p. 162.
40 Himadeh, Ibid., p. 39
41 *Communist Internationalism*, pp. 135–145.
42 Weinstock, Ibid.
43 *Collection*, p.34.
44 The Sublime Porte had granted this land to the Sursuk family of Lebanon in return for services. See also: Hadawi, *Palestine Under the Mandate*. 1920–1948, Palestine Studies, Kuwaiti Alumni Association., pp.34, 36. Likewise, in 1934, the Zionists won the privilege of draining the Al-Houla basin from the Salam family of Beirut, with the help of the Mandate.
45 *Collection*, p.34.
46 Ibid., p.39.
47 Hadawi., p.29.
48 *Collection*, p.25.
49 Ibid., p.56.
50 Ibid., p.58.
51 Himadeh. p.376.
52 *Collection*, p.60.
53 Ibid., pp.62–63.
54 Ibid., p.62.
55 Ibid., p.44.
56 Ibid., p.63.
57 Rony E. Gubbay, *A Political Study of the Arab-Jewish Conflict* (Geneve: Librairie de Droz, 1959), p.29. 109. Sifri, pp.131–132.
58 *Communist Internationalism*, pp.143–144.

Background: The Intellectuals

59 *Collection*, p.52.
60 Himadeh, p.45.
61 "Arab Society" by Dr. Ali Ahmed Issa, quoted in Yusra Arnita, *Folkloric Arts in Palestine*. Beirut, Palestine Research Center, P.L.O. p.187.
62 Dr. Abdul Rahman Yaghi, *Modern Palestinian Literature*, Beirut, p.232.
63 Ibid., p.237.
64 Ibid., p.283.
65 Nimr Sirhan, *Our Popular Songs*, Jordan, Ministry of Culture and Information, p.157.
66 Ibid., pp.299–300.
67 Ibid., p.301.

The Revolution

68 Yehuda Bauer, Op. cit. p.49
69 Issa Sifri, *Arab Palestine Under the Mandate & Zionism*, (Jaffa: the New Palestine Bookshop, Jaffa, 1937), Vol. II p. 10
70 Saleh Bouyissir, *Palestinian Struggle Over Half a Century*, (Beirut: al-Fatah House), p. 180.
71 Subhir Yasine, *The Great Arab Revolution in Palestine*, (Damascus: al-Hana House), p.30

72 Bouyissir, p.181.
73 Kayyali, p.302.
74 *Collection,* p,96.
75 Hadawi, p.38.
76 Subhi Yasine, pp.22-23
77 Ibid. p.22.
78 Kayyali, Op. cit. p.296.
79 *Palestine.* No.94., (Beirut: Arab Higher Committee, Jan 1, 1969).
80 Ibid., No. 94. p.19. *Report by His Majesty's Government in the United Kingdom of Great Britain and Northern Ireland to the Council of the League of Nations on the Administration of Palestine and Trans-Jordan for the Year 1935,* p.8.
81 Kayyali, p.296.
82 *Palestine's Economic Future.* Percy, Lund H. London, 1946. p. 61.
83 Sifri, pp. 39,40.
84 Kayyali, p.311.
85 Sifri, p.60.
86 Ibid., p.93.
87 Kayyali, Op. cit. p.319.
88 *Documents,* p.454.
89 Ibid., p.457.
90 Ibid., p.458.
91 *Collection,* p.8.
92 Kayyali, p.326.
93 Neville Barbour, *Nisi Dominus,* London, pp. 183-193.
94 Kayyali, p.338.
95 *Jewish Observer*, September 20, 1963. London, pp. 13-14.
96 Abdul Qadir Yasin, *al Katib,* No. 121, April 1971 p. 114
97 Kayyali, p.346.
98 Ibid., p.346.
99 Bouyissir, p.247.
100 Ibid., p.247.
101 Ibid., p.258.
102 *Al-Ahram*, March 1, 1939, Cairo.
103 Yasin, Op. cit., p.115.
104 Ibid., p.114.
105 Kayyali, p.359.
106 Anis Sayegh, *The Hashemite & the Palestine Question.* Beirut, 1966, p. 150.
107 Ibid. See also *Al-Talia'a*, No.4 April 7, 1971. Cairo, p. 98.
108 Kayyali, p.348.
109 "A letter from Baghdad to the British Foreign Minister." Oct 31, 1930. Quoted in Kayyali, Ibid. p. 349
110 Walid Khalidi ed, *From Haven to Conquest.* IPS, Beirut, 1971. pp. 836-849.
111 Bouyissir, p.21.
112 Barbour, Op. cit. p.193.

113 Himadeh, p.323.
114 Bouyissir, p.323.
115 Ben-Gurion, p.372.
116 Ibid., p.373.
117 Sifri, Op.cit., pp.131–132.
118 Khalidi, p.375–378.

Afterword

119 Kanafani, *The Revolution*, Op.cit., p.1
120 Ibid., p.2
121 Ibid., p.35
122 Ibid., p.20
123 Ibid., p.36

www.ingramcontent.com/pod-product-compliance
Lightning Source LLC
Chambersburg PA
CBHW031158020426
42333CB00013B/717